101
SUPPORT GROUP ACTIVITIES

For Teenagers Affected by Someone Else's Alcohol/Drug Use

Martin Fleming

HAZELDEN

JOHNSON INSTITUTE

Hazelden
Center City, Minnesota 55012-0176
1-800-328-9000 (Toll Free U.S., Canada, and the Virgin Islands)
1-651-213-4000 (Outside the U.S. and Canada)
1-651-213-4590 (24-hour Fax)
www.hazelden.org

Library of Congress Cataloging-in-Publication Data

Fleming, Martin
        101 support group activities for teenagers affected by someone else's alcohol / drug
use: a leader's manual for secondary educators and other professionals / Martin Fleming.
        p. cm.
        Includes bibliographical references.
        ISBN 13: 1-978-56246-038-9
        1. Children of alcoholics—Counseling of. 2. Group relations training. 3. Self-help groups.
4. Counseling in secondary education. I. Title. II. Title: One hundred one support group activities for
teenagers affected by someone else's alcohol/drug use. III. Title: One hundred and one support group
activities for teenagers affected by someone else's alcohol/drug use.
HV5132.F54 1992   92-9405
362.29'254—dc20   CIP

PRINTED IN THE UNITED STATES OF AMERICA

Acknowledgments

First off, there's Lenore Franzen, my editor and source of clarity and support. I'd also like to thank Jerry Moe for his helpful input and, in particular, four other support group leaders for the activities they shared with me: Shelley Hansen, Jenni Spear, Marilyn North, and Rich Tyler.

Dedication

To my wife, Leigh, my partner in the adventure.

Table of Contents

Section E: Family Relations Activities (69-80)

Introduction

This book is a collection of activities structured around one main goal: to help young people who are affected by someone else's chemical dependence.* Throughout the book, I use the term *parental chemical dependence* for brevity. Of course young people can be affected by, and could be in a support group because of, a sibling's or other relative's chemical dependence.

101 Support Group Activities for Teenagers Affected by Someone Else's Alcohol/Drug Use is primarily a tool for experienced support group leaders who are looking for new and better ways of reaching young people affected by someone else's chemical dependence. Though written with schools in mind, the activities can be readily adapted to a variety of settings: aftercare programs, therapy sessions, treatment centers, youth groups. If you are a beginning support group leader and have more questions than answers at this point, I suggest you read my book *Conducting Support Groups for Students Affected by Chemical Dependence* (Minneapolis: Johnson Institute, 1990). In it you'll learn how to lead support groups and how to integrate them into your school. Being a support group leader can be a challenge and it requires some training and background in chemical dependence. This book won't teach you how to run a support group—it assumes you already know how.

CHEMICAL DEPENDENCE IS A FAMILY DISEASE

Usually when we think of chemical dependence, we most often think of the person who has the disease. It's only recently that we've started to focus on the entire family. Children experiencing chemical dependence in their families also struggle. And that struggle all too often is a silent one. Now, we know about the "Don't talk, don't trust, don't feel" rules in these families. Young people are afraid to reach out and ask for help because of the stigma still associated with a drinking or other drug problem and because they feel as if they would be a traitor to their family. They learn not to trust because of all the unkept promises, the inconsistency and, worst of all, the instances of verbal, physical or sexual abuse to which many are subject. The third rule of "don't feel" naturally follows the first two: This is a painful, messy, confusing, and seemingly hopeless problem, and rather than feel that sharp pain, young people learn how to dull it, how to stuff, deny, or turn off their feelings.

---

*The term "chemical dependence" covers dependence on all mind-altering drugs. Note, too, that the term "alcohol or other drugs" is used throughout this book to emphasize that alcohol is a drug—just like tranquilizers, cocaine, marijuana, heroin, or any other mind-altering substance. Too often people talk about "alcohol or drugs" or "alcohol and drugs" as if alcohol were somehow different from drugs and in a category by itself. True, our culture, our government, even our laws, treat alcohol differently from the way they treat other drugs such as pot, crack, or smack. But the symptoms of dependence are essentially the same for all these mind-altering drugs, and there is an urgent need to find ways to prevent or intervene with their use.

Though each family is unique, most children from chemically dependent families develop responses to the problem that fall into one of four basic patterns. Some children concentrate on making everything perfect, while others act out their feelings in rebellious and destructive ways. Some children withdraw into a world of fantasy, while others use humor and distraction in an attempt to make the problem go away.

But this isn't a problem that will just go away. As evidenced by the growing self-help movement of adult children of alcoholics, children carry their wounds and experiences into adulthood, often either becoming chemically dependent or marrying someone who is chemically dependent. And yet another generation of children affected by parental chemical dependence is in the making.

So when will it ever stop? Fortunately, there are solutions. Support groups are a perfect vehicle for providing the tools and insights that these young people need. Support groups provide great opportunities to connect with peers experiencing similar problems. Support groups facilitate safe, nurturing, and consistent interactions. And support groups provide opportunities for students to begin to understand, share, and cope with uncomfortable feelings.

HOW THIS BOOK IS ORGANIZED

Before each activity is explained, a brief description of a support group in action is provided in chapter 1, curriculum development is outlined in chapter 2, and additional resources are listed in the final section.

The activities themselves are designed for students in grades 7 through 12. But, even though the focus is junior and senior high, many of the activities can be easily adapted for use with younger students. The Resources section (Appendix B) also lists additional curricula specifically geared for young children.

The activities used in support groups help students achieve several goals, including increasing self-esteem, identifying defenses, reducing shame, and learning about the disease of chemical dependence. The activities in this book are divided into eight separate categories:

Group Development activities help a collection of nervous and uncomfortable students become a cohesive and productive group.

Feelings Awareness activities help group members start to identify, understand, share, and cope with their feelings.

Self-exploration activities help group members understand who they are, what they want, and what they need to change.

Chemical Dependence Information activities give information about the disease and how it affects group members as well as their parent with the problem.

Family Relations activities help group members understand the emotional dynamics in their family and what they can do to make things better for themselves.

Movement activities use physical motion rather than talking as a lively way to build group intimacy.

Stress-reduction activities teach group members how to recognize and manage their stress.

Group Challenge activities empower group members to work together as a team.

The techniques for teaching these concepts are varied. Some activities involve discussion, while others incorporate a game. Since many students can express themselves readily through art, many activities challenge students to draw their thoughts and feelings. There are also some activities that use physical motion and noncompetitive games as an avenue for personal growth.

The format for each activity is the same, making it easy for you to use. Goals are listed first, then a brief description, followed by detailed directions on how to carry out the activity. A section called "Notes" reflects what I and other group leaders have learned as we use this activity with kids. Consider it a combination of tips, helpful hints, and suggestions for modifying the activity.

All the necessary worksheets are included for you to copy and distribute in group. When additional materials such as markers or newsprint are required (this manual assumes that students will have a pencil or pen and that there is a blackboard or marker board in the room), I've noted this in the activity. Examples of artwork are also included for clarification. When specific additional information is required for an activity, there is a "For Your Information" section included so that you won't have to hunt down additional resources in order to present the activity.

Accompanying each activity is a brief coding system that identifies the stage, level of challenge, and appropriate grades. "Grades" refers to the academic grades the particular activity is designed for. Note that the term "all" refers to 7 through 12, not grades 1 through 12. "Challenge" describes the degree of intimacy, honesty, or confrontation the activity demands. Activities designated as low challenge are ideal for groups just beginning. Moderately challenging activities will help a support group begin to take the risks necessary to achieve intimacy. Activities with a high level of challenge are often saved for a group that has spent considerable time together. This isn't always the case, though. Sometimes support group leaders, because they have only a few weeks available for the group to meet or because they want to get right to the heart of the matter, will use an activity characterized as a high challenge in the beginning stages of the group. Life Maps (activity #35) is a high-challenge activity you may wish to use as early as the second session because of the intimacy it helps create.

"Stage" refers to the developmental stage for which the specific activity is appropriate. The coding system uses the numbers 1 through 4. The first stage is one of building trust and getting acquainted. Group members need to become comfortable with each other and understand how their group will function concerning rules, goals, and expectations.

In stage 2, the newness is over and now group members need to begin working together. There will be conflict, struggles to define roles, as well as testing of limits and your authority. In stage 3, group members are more comfortable and trusting of each other. It's in this setting that students can begin to take risks and talk about the feelings that they hold so close.

Since all support groups must come to an end, stage 4 describes the process of closure that a group naturally experiences. This should involve more than simply saying good-bye. Stage 4 is a time for students to reflect on what they've learned and experienced as well as to clarify what they'll do differently in the future.

This coding system offers you *guidelines* for selecting activities for your support group. Remember that an activity listed as being appropriate for older students might work very well with a group of mature but younger students, and a stage 3 activity could be modified for use with a fairly new support group.

Above all, as you use these new activities in group, remember that they are simply a medium, a tool, for teaching a concept or creating an opportunity for personal growth. What's really important is our young people and their struggles with the effects of chemical dependence. But, even so, we can't just wave a magic wand or simply tell them not to worry. We must point them down the right path, assisting them in developing their own ideas and insights. So, in this light, the tools are important. A house to keep you safe and warm might be the goal, but it must be built, step by step. These activities are the tools you can use to help students take those steps from despair to hope, from pain to healing.

Chapter One:
For the Beginning Support
Group Leader

Let's look in the window of a support group at work. Students are sitting in a tight circle of comfortable chairs, talking about things important and personal. The coleaders are sitting across from each other, guiding the process as well as participating in the discussion.

The session starts out with a brief warm-up activity to get students focused on their feelings. Then one of the leaders introduces the session topic. After a brief discussion, the students spread out across the floor and begin drawing on large sheets of paper. The adults are drawing as well. Later, the other coleader brings the members back together in a circle and they begin to hold up their drawings, pointing to specific objects and sharing feelings and personal experiences.

At one point, a boy who had been explaining how his father quit playing baseball with him now that he lost his job and started drinking every day begins to cry. The other students move in closer and are quiet, waiting for the boy with the hot, angry tears to continue. When he is finished another student begins, and then another. A few minutes before the session is over, one of the coleaders asks them to put the drawings away and they spend the last minutes talking about what they learned.

Of course, this is merely an example. Support groups change from week to week. And support group leaders have differing styles of running group, too. Controlling or loose, intellectual or with their hearts on their sleeves, confrontive or laid back, the flavor of the group depends on the personality of the leaders as well as the students in the group.

We can control some variables of the group experience, such as the physical qualities of the group room, the number of students in group, and the frequency of the group meetings. Every support group leader must make these decisions based on their own particular situation. Fortunately, collective experience has brought us practical solutions. Here are some typical questions asked by beginning support group leaders and the answers that work in most situations:

HOW MANY STUDENTS SHOULD I HAVE IN MY GROUP?

The maximum number is much more critical than the minimum number. Five to seven students is a good size; eight should be your upper limit. Think about it. Eight students divided by fifty minutes of group works out to six minutes a piece—not much time for a student to talk about her life. But take heart—even when a student isn't speaking there is still much rich learning taking place through group interaction.

IS IT OKAY TO MIX STUDENTS IN A GROUP?

You'll find it helpful to keep the grades separate. Ninth graders, for example, are quite different from seventh grade students in their interaction styles as well as maturity. Mixing genders usually isn't a problem. In fact, it can be beneficial. Balance is important, though. The dynamics can get uncomfortable if, for example, there is only one girl in a group of boys.

HOW OFTEN SHOULD A SUPPORT GROUP MEET?

Typically, groups meet once a week, unless the group is offered for academic credit. Those groups meet every day.

SHOULD GROUPS MEET DURING THE SAME PERIOD EACH SESSION?

While meeting the same period has its advantages—easy for the students to remember, easy for the leaders to prepare—it means that students miss the same class week after week. The best solution is to rotate the group time each week: second period one week, third period next week, and so on.

HOW MANY SESSIONS SHOULD THERE BE?

It would be nice to keep the same group of students together for the entire school year. However, most schools have more students who need group than leaders to lead groups. This means that the greater number of sessions a support group has, the fewer number of students have an opportunity to take part in the group. Most schools tailor the number of sessions to fit in an academic quarter, typically twelve to fourteen sessions.

SHOULD I REQUIRE SIGNED PARENT PERMISSION SLIPS FROM STUDENTS?

This depends on students' ages and the school's policy. Generally speaking, schools must obtain parents' consent for grade-school children to participate in a support group. With junior and senior high students, though, the issue becomes less clear-cut. For example, at what age do young people have the right to exercise a modicum of autonomy when it comes to talking about their feelings, perceptions and problems? Some chemically dependent parents, because of their own denial and fears, often don't want their child to be in a support group. And, because children of a chemically dependent parent anticipate their parent's negative reaction, many students who need a support group the most won't want to be in one.
There are many approaches to this thorny issue:
- offer a support group only to those students who are willing to obtain parental consent
- send a letter to parents at the beginning of the school year that asks them to notify the school if they don't want their children participating in a support group
- describe the group as a communication or self-esteem group, thus reducing the potential for negative parent responses
- simply assert that every student has the right to be in a support group if he or she chooses.

SHOULD MY GROUP MEET DURING OR AFTER SCHOOL?

Definitely during school. Support groups should be viewed as an integral and important part of the school day, not as extracurricular fluff. There are occasions, though, when an after-school program can be appropriate, expecially when community groups such as a Parks and Recreation Department are involved.

WHERE IS A GOOD PLACE TO HOLD GROUP?

The ideal group room is small, carpeted, and equipped with both straight-back chairs and pillows for when the group is on the floor. There shouldn't be any windows, and it should be located in a quiet, low-traffic area. Of course, this is the ideal room, and many group leaders must settle for less. Whatever the room, it's important that it be the same room each session of group. Your last choice should be a standard classroom because of the hard floor, large size, chairs with built-in desks, and impersonal atmosphere.

WHAT SHOULD I CALL MY GROUP?

A popular name is Concerned Persons group. But there are others such as Affected Others group or Insight group. Don't call it a COA group because the "child of an alcoholic" label has powerful connotations attached to it that can be troublesome.

WHAT RULES SHOULD I MAKE FOR MY GROUP?

The fewer the better. Typically rules cover confidentiality, chemical use or possession (No chemicals in you or on you!), and regular attendance. "Everybody must talk about their feelings" is a hope or expectation—don't make it a rule. And don't make rules that you aren't going to enforce consistently. Students get enough of this inconsistency at home. Make your rules specific, reasonable, and enforceable.

SHOULD I HAVE A COLEADER IN MY GROUP?

In a word, yes. Sometimes conditions make it necessary to run group solo, but whenever possible have a helper. Coleaders can come to the rescue when the group gets unmanageable or when you're not picking up on something that a student is feeling. Beginning group leaders should always have the assistance of a seasoned pro.

WHERE DO I DRAW THE LINE WITH GROUP CONFIDENTIALITY?

Generally speaking, anything that a student says in group stays in group. But, in situations of abuse (physical or sexual), harming one's self (suicide), or harming others (assault or homicide), you must report this information. These exceptions to the confidentiality rule should be explained during the first session of group.

The above merely touches on some rather complex and thorny issues surrounding the reality of support groups in a school setting. Again, if you are contemplating initiating a support group in your school, you need more information and training. *Conducting Support Groups for Students Affected by Chemical Dependence* will assist you in developing the framework necessary for support groups to function effectively.

Chapter Two: Designing A Curriculum

With a skilled leader, a single group session has a carefully orchestrated flow from beginning to end. And in the bigger picture, so, too, does an entire group curriculum. Rather than being put together in a random fashion, group activities should be in a specific sequence that encourages learning and growth. This chapter outlines the five key steps for designing your own group curriculum.

STEP 1

Your first task as a group leader is to decide on the total number of sessions your group will meet. Most Concerned Persons groups have a total of eight to fourteen sessions. If your group meets weekly, then this fits comfortably into an average school quarter, while leaving time to meet with students referred to group at the beginning of the quarter and won't interfere with quarterly tests.

STEP 2

Once you decide how many times your group will meet, it's tempting to begin planning what you'll do during those sessions. Stop right there! First select your group goals. Just as the carpenter first draws up the house plan and then makes a list of tools she will need to build this house, first make a list of the goals you would like to meet in your support group. Don't be concerned yet with a specific order. Example 2.1 will help get you started with your own list.

STEP 3

Most likely, you will have listed more goals than can be realistically addressed in the time constraints of a typical support group. You'll need to prioritize. (I've found that the least painful way to whittle down this list is to begin crossing out the least-important goals first.) How many goals can you realistically try to address in your support group? As a general guideline, you shouldn't have more goals than you do sessions of group. Actually, since virtually every support group's initial session is used to discuss the rules of the group and reduce students' uneasiness and the final session is set aside for closure, your number of goals should be the total number of sessions minus two. Which goals are the most important to address in a support group? Here are the basic categories of goals that are common to nearly all support group curricula:

Education—teach students about chemical dependence.

Feelings—help students learn how to recognize, understand, express, and cope with their feelings.

Self-worth—help students feel better about themselves, assert their personal power and autonomy, and feel validated.

Coping—teach problem-solving skills and offer practical solutions.

Linking—Encourage sense of community, reaching out to others, improved family relations, and need for on-going support.

STEP 4

Once you have made a grocery list of goals, it's time to find corresponding activities. This is the fun part. Page through the sections in this book and select activities that both meet your identified goals and are appropriate for the students in your group. You should choose one activity for each goal on your list. Don't be afraid to try new activities—you might be pleasantly surprised. You may want to have a back-up activity ready in case the first one doesn't work as planned.

STEP 5

Now that you have a goal and a corresponding activity for each session of group, it's time to place these activities in a sequence that's most helpful to the group members. Generally speaking, the initial sessions should be used to calm nerves and reduce tension. The middle sessions are the meat of the group, introducing new concepts, breaking down resistance, and promoting self-awareness. The final sessions of group recap learning and facilitate closure. Example 2.2 is a worksheet that will guide you through all five steps of the planning process.

For those of you who, at this point, would rather stick with a curriculum that has been field-tested and proven to work well, I've included several options in Example 2.3. Feel free to follow these exactly or modify them to meet your specific needs. The Resources section also lists several sources of group curricula.

Example 2.1: Group Goals

- Teach students the dynamics of chemical use, abuse, and dependence.
- Teach students the disease concept of chemical dependence.
- Help students feel better about themselves.
- Validate students' experiences.
- Teach students that they aren't responsible for the problem.
- Help students identify, understand, and express their feelings.
- Build self-confidence and self-esteem.
- Confront students' denial.
- Help students build a personal support system.
- Inform students of their high risk for becoming chemically dependent.
- Help students learn how to have fun.
- Teach stress-management techniques.
- Provide opportunities for students to help their peers.
- Create a safe place to talk about feelings.
- Offer the students stable relationships with adults.
- Help students identify what they need for themselves.
- Help students realize that they aren't the only ones with this problem.
- Help students improve their relationships with family members.
- Strengthen coping skills.
- Take responsibility for their own recovery programs.
- Teach healthy decision-making skills.
- Help them find ways to deal with their painful feelings.
- Help students identify, understand, and change their enabling behaviors.
- Develop competency with age-appropriate tasks.
- Strengthen relationship with non-chemically dependent parent.
- Improve academic performance.
- Develop nurturing relationships with school staff members.
- Help school staff gain insight into a student's problems.
- Encourage students to use community support resources.
- Help students begin to trust others.
- Encourage intimacy and bonding within the support group.
- Facilitate termination of the group experience.

Example 2.2: Curriculum Planning Worksheet

STEP 1:

How many sessions will your group have?_____

STEP 2:

Make a list of goals for your group:

STEP 3:

Select one goal for each session except the first and last.

STEP 4:
Select a group activity for each goal.

Goal	Activity
_____	_____
_____	_____
_____	_____
_____	_____
_____	_____
_____	_____
_____	_____
_____	_____
_____	_____
_____	_____
_____	_____
_____	_____
_____	_____
_____	_____
_____	_____
_____	_____
_____	_____

STEP 5:
Organize the goals and the corresponding activities in a constructive sequence:

Session #	Goal	Activity
_____	_____	_____
_____	_____	_____
_____	_____	_____
_____	_____	_____
_____	_____	_____
_____	_____	_____
_____	_____	_____
_____	_____	_____
_____	_____	_____
_____	_____	_____
_____	_____	_____
_____	_____	_____
_____	_____	_____

Example 2.3:
Curriculum Examples

EXAMPLE A:	This twelve-session group curriculum works well with most students. The Life Maps activity uses four sessions, but you'll find it an invaluable method for developing group intimacy and for encouraging students to open up and begin talking about what's really important.

SESSION 1

INTRODUCTIONS
Goals: Establish group rapport
         Explain group rules and goals
Activity: Interview Exercise (Activity #3)

SESSION 2-5

PERSONAL HISTORY
Goals: Validate personal experiences
         Establish group unity
Activity: Life Maps (Activity # 35)

SESSION 6

FEELINGS
Goal: Increase awareness of feelings
         Develop communication skills
Activity: My Own Feelings (Activity #19)

SESSION 7

DEFENSES
Goal: Identify personal defenses
Activity: My Two Sides (Activity #18)

SESSION 8

CHEMICAL DEPENDENCE INFORMATION
Goal: Teach chemical dependence concepts
Activity: Four Phases of Chemical Dependence (Activity #49)

SESSION 9

DETACHING FROM THE PROBLEM
Goal: Learn detachment skills
Activity: Detaching from the Problem (Activity #64)

SESSION 10

PERSONAL NEEDS
Goal: Identify personal needs
Activity: My Own Needs (Activity #47)

SESSION 11

FUTURE PLANS
Goal: Reinforce previous learning experiences
Activity: From Now On (Activity #27)

SESSION 12

CLOSURE
Goal: Facilitate group closure
Activity: Warm Fuzzy Bags (Activity #14)

EXAMPLE B:

This curriculum is designed for younger students. The activities focus on basic concepts and use drawing, movement, and simple lists rather than discussion or lecture. The eight sessions make it possible to complete two cycles of group within a typical school quarter of eighteen weeks.

SESSION 1

INTRODUCTIONS
Goals: Establish group rapport
              Explain group goals and rules
Activity: Take What You Need (Activity #4)

SESSION 2

FEELINGS
Goals: Increase awareness of feelings
              Develop communication skills
Activity: Foot Faces (Activity #20)

SESSION 3

CHEMICAL DEPENDENCE INFORMATION
Goal: Teach chemical dependence concepts
Activity: Four Phases of Chemical Dependence (Activity #49)

SESSION 4

DEFENSES
Goal: Identify personal defenses
Activity: Paper Bag People (Activity #24)

SESSION 5

FAMILY RELATIONS
Goal: Increase understanding of family dynamics
Activity: Family Faces (Activity #69)

SESSION 6

COPING
Goal: Develop coping skills
Activity: Taking Care of Me (Activity #62)

SESSION 7

SELF-ESTEEM
Goal: Increase self-esteem
Activity: Five Great Things about Me (Activity #40)

SESSION 8

CLOSURE
Goal: Facilitate group closure
Activity: Spine Graffiti (Activity #7)

EXAMPLE C:

This curriculum is appropriate for students in grades ten through twelve. After introducing basic chemical dependence concepts and looking at family dynamics, this sequence explores a variety of personal issues. Note that session eight encourages group members to evaluate their own chemical use since many students, by this age, will have begun experimenting with chemicals and are at high risk for becoming chemically dependent themselves.

SESSION 1

INTRODUCTIONS
Goals: Establish group rapport
           Explain group goals and rules
Activity: Five Things We Have in Common (Activity #9)

SESSION 2

CHEMICAL DEPENDENCE INFORMATION
Goal: Teach chemical dependence concepts
Activity: The Disease Called Chemical Dependence (Activity #48)

SESSION 3

FAMILY RELATIONS
Goal: Increase understanding of family dynamics
Activity: Family Collage (Activity #71)

SESSION 4

FEELINGS
Goal: Encourage healthy management of feelings
Activity: What Should I Do with My Feelings? (Activity #23)

SESSION 5

STRESS
Goal: Teach stress management
Activity: Stress Reduction Through Relaxation (Activity #93)

SESSION 6

SUPPORT SYSTEM
Goals: Assess personal relationships
           Increase level of support
Activity: Connections Map (Activity #33)

SESSION 7

TRUST
Goal: Increase awareness of trust issues
Activity: Trust Falls (Activity #84)

SESSION 8

CHEMICAL DEPENDENCE INFORMATION
Goal: Assess students' chemical use
Activity: My Own Chemical Use (Activity #66)

SESSION 9

GOALS
Goal: Encourage goal setting
Activity: Goals and Decisions (Activity #29)

SESSION 10

CLOSURE
Goal: Facilitate group closure
Activity: Support Group Party (Activity #101)

The Activities

Section A:
Group Development Activities

This first section will transform students sitting nervously in a circle of chairs into an intimate, trusting, and productive support group. A tall order? Not really. Actually, you'll find that after getting the young people to come to the initial group session, you're already halfway home. Remember, they want to talk about their pain, lessen their burdens, and get some answers.

But most of these students don't know how to work together as a team, let alone how a support group functions. They're used to going it alone with their feelings and struggles. Isolation and pretending are the name of their game, while support groups encourage just the opposite. Though not a word has been said about chemical dependence, all of the activities in this first section are important because they build a secure foundation upon which more challenging activities can be presented. Breaking the ice, building themes of commonality, encouraging students to support each other, and providing transitions to and from the "real world" outside of group are all bricks carefully laid for the structure yet to come.

1
Warm-ups

GOALS: ▶

- Provide a transition from a cognitive to an affective learning mode
- Help students focus on group process
- Energize a lethargic group

DESCRIPTION: ▶

Warm-ups are brief activities used during the first few minutes of group to help students focus on their feelings and group process.

DIRECTIONS: ▶

When first introducing this activity, you should select the warm-up question and pose it to the group. After that, appoint a different group member to select and initiate the warm-up question for each subsequent session. Group members may either make up their own question or choose one from the list you provide (see following page). This activity isn't the mainstay of a group session; it's simply a way to become focused on group process—not unlike a runner stretching before a workout. Five minutes is an adequate amount of time for this activity.

NOTES: ▶

In order to place more responsibility on the group, you could ask the student in charge of the Warm-up for the current session to assign next session's Warm-up to another group member. This process can then continue each session of group.

MATERIALS: ▶

Warm-up questions.

Warm-up Questions

- Name a feeling that's easy for you to talk about. Why?

- Name a feeling that's difficult for you to talk about. Why?

- Are you more like your mother or your father? Why?

- Communicate nonverbally how you are feeling.

- When somebody hurts your feelings, what do you do?

- What do you do when you are angry?

- Tell the group one thing that you appreciate about yourself.

- After everyone is sitting in a tight circle, have them turn to their right and massage their neighbor's neck.

- If you were an animal, what type would you be? Why?

- Demonstrate your personality when you were a little child.

- Name one physical quality about yourself that you like.

- Identify one quality that you have to offer a friend.

- When was the last time you cried? What were the tears about?

- When you really need to talk to somebody, who do you turn to?

- What is one thing that people don't understand about you?

- When you need alone time, where do you go and what do you do?

2
Cool-downs

GOALS: ▶
- Provide closure for group activities
- Clarify learning

DESCRIPTION: ▶ Cool-downs are brief activities that bring a raw or unfinished group session to closure and reinforce learning.

DIRECTIONS: ▶ Reserve the last five minutes or so of each group session for this activity. Choose a sentence stem from the following page, appropriate to the activity the group has just finished, and ask group members to respond.

NOTES: ▶ When a group session hasn't been very intense, you probably won't need a closing activity. You may wish to leave it up to the group to decide. You could also ask group members to choose the closing question.

MATERIALS: ▶ List of **Cool-downs.**

Cool-downs List

- Ask group members what they learned about themselves today.

- Tell a joke.

- Ask everyone to get up and stretch.

- Hold hands and be silent for two minutes.

- Tell the group members something you appreciate about them.

- Ask a member of the group to summarize what happened during the group.

- Ask group members to tell a person in group who is having an especially difficult time something they appreciate about her.

- Ask group members what they need from the rest of the group.

- Ask the group what they would like to do next week.

- Ask group members if they have anything they would like to say to the rest of the group.

3
Interview Exercise

GOALS:

- Establish group rapport
- Ease tension in a beginning group

DESCRIPTION:

Group members interview each other and then introduce their partner to the rest of the group.

DIRECTIONS:

Pair members of the group together—preferably with someone they don't know very well—and instruct them to ask each other the questions on the worksheet you've handed out (see following page). Position these diads around the group room so that they have a little privacy. The interviewer should write his partner's answers on his own sheet next to the questions. When the interviewer is finished asking questions, the pair should reverse roles. After everybody has finished, bring them back into a circle and ask each person to introduce his or her partner to the group and share the recorded responses.

NOTES:

Depending on the time remaining in the session, ask follow-up questions to the students' answers—"Oh, so you like rock climbing. Where do you go to do that?" for example. This will both encourage discussion as well as help group members to feel valued and important.

MATERIALS:

Interview Exercise worksheet.

Interview

Ask your partner these questions and write their answers next to the questions on your sheet.

1. What is your name?

2. Where were you born?

3. What do you like to do in your spare time?

4. What is something that really bugs you?

5. If you had five thousand dollars, what would you do with it?

6. What is your favorite music group?

7. What one word would best describe you?

8. What are you looking forward to this year?

9. What aren't you looking forward to this year?

10. What are you afraid of?

Now, think of two additional questions to ask your partner:

11. Question:

     Answer:

12. Question:

     Answer:

4
Take What You Need

GOALS:

- Encourage self-disclosure
- Reduce communication barriers

DESCRIPTION:

Group members volunteer information about themselves in whatever areas they choose.

DIRECTIONS:

Place a container of M&Ms or a roll of toilet paper in the center of the group circle. Tell group members to take what they need. At this point, don't give any further instructions. After everyone has taken what they want, tell the group that everyone must share one thing about themselves for each M&M or sheet of toilet paper they have taken. Go around the circle as many times as are required. Group members should be encouraged to share anything they wish.

NOTES:

If you use M&Ms, it would be a good idea to limit the amount you place in the circle. Otherwise some students could grab such a large handful that they would need several hours of sharing time!

MATERIALS:

M&Ms or toilet paper.

5
Sentence Stems

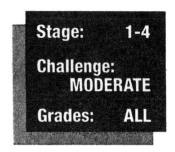

GOALS:
- Encourage honest communication
- Allow students to determine the session's focus

DESCRIPTION: ►
Group members take turns choosing and completing sentence stems.

DIRECTIONS: ►
Distribute copies of the **Sentence Stems** worksheet (see following page) and ask each group member to choose and then complete each phrase in turn. After a student answers, the rest of the group can ask for more information or clarification. Tell the group they can make up their own phrase sentence stems if they can't find one on the sheet that they like.

NOTES: ►
Give everyone a copy of the sentence stems, so time isn't wasted while students read through the list looking for a phrase to complete. A variation of this activity would be to ask the person who just answered a question to choose the sentence stem for the next group member.

MATERIALS: ►
Sentence Stems worksheet.

Sentence Stems

1. Right now I'm feeling . . .
2. When I'm alone I feel . . .
3. When I'm surrounded by people I feel . . .
4. One thing that I hate is . . .
5. One thing that I really like about myself is . . .
6. When I'm feeling sad I . . .
7. The last time I cried was . . .
8. When I daydream it's usually about . . .
9. I'm afraid of . . .
10. I'm the happiest when . . .
11. One thing that really worries me is . . .
12. If I could change one thing about myself it would be . . .
13. If I could be with anyone right now I would be with . . .
14. The family member I'm closest to is . . .
15. If I was really honest with my father I would tell him . . .
16. One thing I regret about my life is . . .
17. If I only had one more day to live I would . . .
18. If I was really honest with my mother I would tell her . . .
19. One thing about me that nobody knows is . . .
20. I hope that someday in the future . . .
21. When I think about my family I feel . . .
22. Something I feel really embarrassed about is . . .
23. One thing about me I never want to change is . . .
24. One thing I feel really proud of is . . .
25. This support group has helped me to . . .
26. One thing I like about all of you is . . .

6
Ask the Question

GOALS: ▶

- Encourage discussion of important and relevant issues
- Increase the trust level of the group

DESCRIPTION: ▶

Group members take turns asking each other questions relevant to the group experience.

DIRECTIONS: ▶

Explain to the group that the purpose of this activity is to find out more about each other and to encourage discussion of issues that are important but sometimes difficult to talk about. Begin by asking the first question directed to a single group member. The person who answers your question creates the next question and decides whom she would like to answer it. If the person being asked the question doesn't wish to answer he can simply say "pass." In this case, the person asking the question can then choose a new group member.

NOTES: ▶

As long as the questions don't get too ridiculous or unproductive, resist the temptation to jump in and take charge. Group members need to work this out on their own.

MATERIALS: ▶

None required.

7
Spine Graffiti

GOALS:
- Give and receive compliments within the group
- Increase self-esteem

DESCRIPTION:
Students give compliments to each other anonymously.

DIRECTIONS:
Pass out sheets of paper, masking tape, and enough crayons for everyone. Explain to the group that they will be walking around the room with a sheet of paper taped to their backs and that they are to write compliments and other positive thoughts on each other's back, such as "You are very warm and friendly," "You have really beautiful brown eyes," or "I trust you." When everyone is finished, they can take the papers off their backs and read what has been written.

NOTES:
If group members wish, they may sign their names to their compliments.

MATERIALS:
Sheets of paper, crayons, masking tape.

8
One Thing I Like About You

GOALS: ▶
- Encourage giving and receiving compliments
- Allow students to take risks in a safe environment
- Increase self-esteem

DESCRIPTION: ▶ Each group member gives a compliment to one group member who is chosen to be the focus of attention. Every student is given the opportunity to receive compliments from the rest of the group.

DIRECTIONS: ▶ Discuss the importance of self-esteem with the group, pointing out that though it's sometimes embarrassing to be given compliments, it sure makes us feel good. And it's important to feel good about ourselves, that we matter, that we have something to offer.

Choose someone to be the center of attention and then proceed around the circle, asking everybody to give a compliment to this particular student. When all have shared something, pick someone else (or ask for volunteers) to be the focus and repeat the sharing until everyone has had a chance to be the center of attention.

After everyone has received compliments, discuss the group members' reactions to being the focus of so many compliments. Encourage them to think about how they typically react to compliments they receive from family and friends.

QUESTIONS: ▶
- How did it feel to be given these compliments?
- Was it harder to give them or to receive them?
- Would it be okay to ask friends or family to give you some compliments when you are feeling down? Why or why not?

NOTES: ▶ This isn't an activity for a group in its beginning stages. In fact, this activity won't even work in some groups that have been meeting for a long time because of the personal risk involved. When this activity does work, though, it's wonderfully effective at providing an avenue for group members to give each other sincere and powerful compliments.

MATERIALS: ▶ None required.

9
Five Things We Have in Common

GOALS:

- Establish group rapport
- Encourage honest communication

DESCRIPTION:

Group members break into teams of two or three, and find five things that they all share in common.

DIRECTIONS:

Depending on the number of students in the group, divide the students into teams of two or three. Instruct them to discover something that each member of the team shares in common. This could be age, owning a dog, or liking the same music. After the team has found this commonality, ask them to repeat the task, but this time give them a focus, such as characteristics of parents, things they're afraid of, or feelings they don't like dealing with, for example. Each time you repeat the task, make the specific focus more difficult and personal.

NOTES:

You may wish to shift team members at some point in this activity so that students have a chance to get to know other group members.

MATERIALS:

None required.

10
Guess Who I Am?

GOALS: ▶
- Encourage honest communication
- Identify inaccurate self-perceptions
- Increase self-esteem

DESCRIPTION: ▶
Students write two brief personality sketches—the first concerning how they view themselves, the second how they think the rest of the group views them. After guessing the correct identity of the sketches, the group discusses the second sketches.

DIRECTIONS: ▶
Ask group members to write brief personality sketches about themselves. This short, one or two paragraph sketch should describe their mannerisms, how they interact with others, common moods, likes and dislikes, and so on. Once they've finished the first sketch, ask them to write another similar sketch on the bottom half of the paper, but this second sketch should focus on how they think the rest of the support group views them. In short, what do they think other students in the group think about them.

Once everyone has finished writing, collect the sketches and mix them up in a stack. Read the first sketch in the pile out loud to the group and ask them to guess who they think is the author. After everyone has guessed, identify the person who wrote the sketch and then read the second part—how this person thinks the rest of the group sees her—to the group. As you read this second sketch, pause after each specific point and ask the group if they agree or disagree. For example, if this group member wrote, "My support group thinks I am shy and quiet" ask the group if they agree: "Do all of you see Kathy as shy and quiet?"

After reading the entire second sketch, ask the group to make additions to the sketch that the author didn't include—"Well, Kathy didn't say anything about how she always tries to help other people in the group when they are feeling down," for example. Follow this same routine for every group members' set of personality sketches.

MATERIALS:
Paper.

11
Eavesdropping

GOALS:
- Discover new solutions to students' problems
- Encourage feedback from the group

DESCRIPTION: ▶
One group member sits outside the circle while the remainder of the group discusses his problems and possible solutions within his hearing distance.

DIRECTIONS: ▶
After explaining this activity to the group, ask for a volunteer. Inform the group that everyone will get a turn. Ask the volunteer to take her chair and sit some five feet outside the group circle with her back to the group. Tell her that she can listen to the conversation within the group, but that she can't respond until after they're finished and invite her back to the circle.

Now, with her removed from the circle, ask the rest of the group to discuss this person: her family situation, the things about her that they appreciate, the things about her that concern them, what they think she should do to improve her situation.

When they are finished, ask her to rejoin the circle, allowing her to respond to the group's suggestions if she wishes. Discourage defensive justifications, however, reminding her that this is simply opinions of other group members and she is free (as they say in a number of twelve-step programs) to take what she likes and leave the rest.

Use the rest of the session for other group members to be the focus of attention.

NOTES:
You may wish to place the student being discussed behind a screen. This additional anonymity for the rest of the group encourages them to share their thoughts honestly. At times you may need to steer the conversation back towards a constructive focus if group members make inappropriate comments in an attempt to be humorous.

MATERIALS:
None required.

12
A Pat on the Back

GOALS: ▶
- Understand the importance of self-esteem
- Practice giving and receiving strokes
- Help students begin to value themselves

DESCRIPTION: ▶

Group members give each other and themselves positive self-esteem messages using a prop that simulates being patted on the back.

DIRECTIONS: ▶

First, make the dummy arm. This arm can be made out of cardboard, or the entire arm of a shirt stuffed with rags and fitted with a cardboard hand. Attach the shoulder end of the arm to a belt so that when you put on the belt, the arm is positioned in the middle of your back. Attach a string onto the wrist of the arm. Put on the belt, throw the string over your shoulder, and pull. There you have it . . . a pat on the back!

Before playing this game, introduce the concept of self-esteem—getting pats on the back—by using the prop. Ask group members for examples of messages that others give them that help them to feel good about themselves. Explain to the group that you can also give yourself these self-esteem messages. Ask the group for examples.

Once this concept is well understood, give a group member a turn with the dummy arm. Have him stand in the center of the group circle and attach the arm to his back. Ask members of the group to give him positive messages that will help boost his self-esteem, such as "I really like the way you help everyone out in group," "You have a great laugh," or "You have always been very honest." Each time a group member gives him a positive stroke, the person with the arm must also give himself a positive stroke out loud. And with each stroke the dummy arm should be patting him on the back. When a student's turn is finished, allow him to pick another member of the group to be next in the center.

QUESTIONS: ▶
- Is it easier to give or receive strokes?
- What feelings are associated with giving or receiving strokes?
- Do we need strokes in order to be happy?

NOTES: ▶

This particular activity can be accomplished without the dummy arm, but, especially with younger students, the arm serves to reinforce the concept.

MATERIALS: ▶

Cardboard, an old shirt, string, a belt.

13
What Do We Have in Common?

Stage: 1-2

Challenge: LOW

Grades: ALL

GOALS:
- Explore commonalities of group members
- Encourage group unity

DESCRIPTION:
Group members discover things they share in common by making groupings around various themes such as eye color, birth month, and favorite food.

DIRECTIONS:
Tell the group that the purpose of this activity is to discover how many different ways the group shares things in common. Start by asking them to form groupings based on eye color. Once these groups have been formed (let them figure out how to actually do this), ask a group member to choose another grouping such as number of siblings, birth month, color of shoes, and so on. Other than making sure everyone gets a chance to determine the grouping, let the students take responsibility for making this game work.

NOTES:
After the group has exhausted groupings, you might challenge them to discover commonalities related to the issue of chemical dependence, such as gender of the chemically dependent parent, chemical of choice for this parent, or whether this person has gone through treatment.

MATERIALS:
None required.

14
Warm Fuzzy Bags

GOALS: ▶
- Facilitate group closure
- Allow expression of feelings between group members

DESCRIPTION: ▶
Group members write thoughts and feelings on slips of paper for all members in the group.

DIRECTIONS: ▶
Hand out paper lunch bags for everyone to decorate with markers. While they are doing this, explain to the group that warm fuzzies are compliments and things they say to each other that make the other person feel good. Discuss examples of warm fuzzies, such as "You have a great personality," "Thanks for all the support in group," and "I learned a lot from you." Then give everyone enough slips of paper so they can write a warm fuzzy for each person in group, putting the slip of paper in the students' bag when they are done.

NOTES: ▶
The warm fuzzies can be anonymous if group members prefer not to sign their names. You might also ask them to write a warm fuzzy to themselves from themselves.

MATERIALS: ▶
Materials: Paper lunch bags, slips of paper equaling the number of group members multiplied by itself and markers.

15
Group Evaluations

GOALS: ▶
- Solicit feedback from students about their group experiences
- Improve the effectiveness of support groups for future students
- Collect data regarding the impact of the group experience

DESCRIPTION: ▶ Group members complete written anonymous evaluations of their group experience.

DIRECTIONS: ▶ Hand out the **Group Evaluation** worksheets (see following page), stressing to group members that they shouldn't write their names on the evaluations and that they should answer the questions honestly. Let them know that their feedback will be used to make the group experience better next time around for new students who join a support group.

NOTES: ▶ There are several different ways in which you can get these evaluations completed by group members, each having their own benefits and drawbacks. Perhaps the most popular and obvious way is to reserve the last ten minutes of the final group session to complete the worksheets. The drawback to this method is that this is a time when the group is feeling very emotional and intimate, and then you give them paperwork to complete (think about how much you detest writing evaluations after a long workshop). Instead, you could hand the worksheets out as they are leaving and ask them to return them when they are finished, but some students will forget or lose their worksheets. In this case, if there is academic credit being given for group attendance, you could reserve the final credit until the evaluations have been returned.

MATERIALS: ▶ **Group Evaluation** worksheets.

Group Evaluation

Please take a minute to fill out this group evaluation. Do not put your name on it. Thank you.

1. Was your group a valuable experience for you?

   No   Maybe   Yes
   1   2   3   4   5   6   7   8   9   10

2. How would you rate your group leaders' ability to lead group?

   Poor   Excellent

   1   2   3   4   5   6   7   8   9   10

3. How helpful were your group leaders for you?

   group leader's name_____   group leader's name _____

   Of little help   Very helpful   Of little help   Very helpful

   1   2   3   4   5   6   7   8   9   10   1   2   3   4   5   6   7   8   9   10

4. List three things that you learned in group.

1)

2)

3)

5. How did this group help you?

6. How could this group be improved?

Section B: Feelings Awareness Activities

Feelings are truly the foundation of a support group. Many students with chemically dependent parents, having grown up in an environment where feelings aren't acknowledged or resolved in healthy ways, lack even the most basic feelings skills. Often, they don't know how to identify their own feelings beyond the mad, sad, and glad level.

Because of this painful environment, these young people have a well-developed set of defenses. Unfortunately, walls built for personal protection can become walls of a personal jail, keeping them from resolving painful feelings as well as preventing them from reaching out to safe people for support. Just as chemically dependent people have a rigid system of defenses, so too can affected family members.

Once these students learn about their feelings and begin to share them, there's yet another task. They must learn how to deal with their feelings in healthy ways. This isn't something that they are accustomed to doing. After all, consider their role models: Dad gets drunk when he's angry and Mom hides her pain with a frozen smile. Fortunately, when we provide a safe place, an activity that isn't too challenging, and the feeling vocabulary, these students will begin to thaw out and open up, as well as discover new ways to cope with whatever feelings come their way. This section encourages this process.

16
Ten Different Feelings

GOALS: ▶
- Identify personal defenses
- Encourage discussion of secret feelings

DESCRIPTION: ▶
Group members use a worksheet to categorize feelings that are easy to share with others and feelings that are difficult to share with others.

DIRECTIONS: ▶
Ask group members to list some feelings that are easy to talk about; then ask them to list feelings that are really hard to talk about. Once familiar with this distinction, pass out the **Ten Different Feelings** worksheet (see following page). After they've had time to complete the worksheet, go around the circle and ask group members to share what they've written. Time permitting, ask them to relate an instance when they used a defense to cover up a feeling listed on their worksheet.

MATERIALS: ▶
Ten Different Feelings worksheet.

Ten Different Feelings

In the blanks provided, write in ten different feelings.

Then next to each feeling word you wrote, tell why the feeling is easy or difficult to talk about with other people.

■ Five feelings easy for me to talk about with others are:

1: _____

2: _____

3: _____

4: _____

5: _____

■ Five feelings difficult for me to talk about with others are:

1: _____

2: _____

3: _____

4: _____

5: _____

17
Feelings Chart

GOALS: ▶
- Expand student's feelings vocabulary
- Create a visual aid for future group sessions
- Encourage teamwork

DESCRIPTION: ▶ Group members create a poster for the group room, listing a variety of feelings.

DIRECTIONS: ▶ Remind group members that sometimes it's difficult to name exactly a feeling you're experiencing. Tell them that you'd like them to make a poster that lists all the different feeling words they know, and that they can refer to it when they need help naming a feeling.

First, using a blackboard or flip chart, ask them to think of all the feeling words they know. Once there is a comprehensive list, then they should decide on a grouping and ordering strategy. For example, they might want to place all of the angry feeling words together (see Appendix A on page 180 for a comprehensive list of feelings).

Then ask them to record these feelings on a large sheet of posterboard. If there are some artistic students in the group, it can be helpful to sketch a small, simple face next to the word that demonstrates the feeling. Encourage them to be creative through use of different colors, layout style, and word order (see following page).

NOTES: ▶ Once this feelings poster is finished, you can refer to it whenever a student is struggling to name a feeling. If a question has been posed to the group regarding how they're feeling about something in particular, and a student responds, "I don't know," you can refer her to the poster, asking, "Can you find the feeling up there?"

MATERIALS: ▶ Posterboard, markers, paints, and brushes.

Afraid	Anxious	Bitter	Bored	Cautious	Confident
Disappointed	Discouraged	Eager	Enraged	Envious	Excited
Frightened	Frustrated	Glad	Guilty	Happy	Horrified
Hurt	Inadequate	Insecure	Jealous	Joyful	Lonely
Loved	Mad	Miserable	Obstinate	Optimistic	Paranoid
Perplexed	Powerless	Resentful	Relieved	Sad	Satisfied
Shocked	Tense	Uneasy	Unsure	Worried	Worthwhile

18
My Two Sides

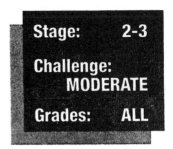

GOALS: ▶
- Identify personal defenses
- Encourage discussion of secret feelings

DESCRIPTION: ▶
Group members explore the differences between their public and private feelings by labeling these feelings on an outline of their body.

DIRECTIONS: ▶
Ask group members to draw a large outline shape of themselves on newsprint. If the newsprint is large enough, they can lie down on the paper and have a friend trace their body on the paper. Inside the figure they should detail the feelings they keep to themselves and outside the figure, the feelings they reveal to the world around them. After everyone has done this, the disparity between the inside and outside should be discussed.

QUESTIONS: ▶
- What feelings do you have hidden inside?
- How do you present yourself to your family? to your friends?
- Why is there a difference between your inside feelings and your outside feelings?
- Why are some feelings harder to share than others?

NOTES: ▶
If you are instructing group members to draw their actual body outlines, be sensitive to possible uncomfortable feelings of a group member who is overweight or underweight.

MATERIALS: ▶
Large sheets of newsprint or bulletin board paper and markers.

19
My Own Feelings

GOALS: ▶
- Increase awareness of feelings
- Develop communication skills

DESCRIPTION: ▶ Group members use a worksheet to help them identify different feelings they've experienced. Afterwards, group members share their answers with the rest of the group.

DIRECTIONS: ▶ Begin this session by asking the students to name as many feelings as they can, including an example of what the particular feeling word means. Then ask the students to complete the **My Own Feelings** worksheet (see following page). After they have finished, go around the circle and ask each group member to share with the rest of the group what he has written.

NOTES: ▶ Some group members might have a difficult time identifying with all but a few feelings. When this is the case, be prepared to offer examples or, better yet, ask the group to name a few examples of the particular feeling.

MATERIALS: ▶ **My Own Feelings** worksheet.

My Own Feelings

There are five feelings listed below. For each feeling listed, think of a time you have felt that way. On the bottom of the sheet there are two blanks for you to write in two other feelings you have experienced.

A time I felt **angry** was:

A time I felt **happy** was:

A time I felt **scared** was:

A time I felt **sad** was:

A time I felt **guilty** was:

A time I felt _____ was:

A time I felt _____ was:

20
Foot Faces

GOALS:

- Create awareness of past feelings
- Encourage honest discussion of feelings

DESCRIPTION: ▶

Students draw several outlines of their feet and turn them into faces representing various periods of their lives.

DIRECTIONS: ▶

Pass around large sheets of newsprint and ask group members to stand on the sheets and draw the outline of their feet. They should do this several times so that they have at least six foot outlines. When they are finished, ask them to think of different times in their lives when they remember feeling specific feelings: angry when a friend turned against them, lonely when they moved to a new town, afraid because a parent was drinking heavily, sad when their parents got divorced. Ask them to write a short note for each of these memories next to a foot outline—one memory for each foot outline. The notations could be as simple as the name of the friend who turned against them, the name of the new town, or the word "divorce." Once this is done ask group members to turn each foot outline into a face by drawing in the facial expressions appropriate for the experience described next to the foot. When everyone has finished, ask them to share their foot faces and the experiences that brought about these different feelings.

MATERIALS:

Large sheets of newsprint and markers.

21
Spin the Bottle

Stage: 2-3

Challenge: HIGH

Grades: ALL

GOALS:

- Increase feelings awareness
- Encourage communication in group

DESCRIPTION: ▶

Group members spin a bottle to select who is "it." This person draws from a stack of feelings cards and describes the last time he felt the particular feeling named on the card.

PROCEDURE: ▶

Make a number of 3 x 5 inch cards that have a feeling word written on each one (see Appendix A for list of feelings). Place a pop bottle in the center of the circle. Have a student spin the bottle to start the game. Whomever the bottle points to must draw a card from the top of the deck and tell the group the last time she felt this particular feeling and explain the circumstances. After she's finished, she puts the card on the bottom of the deck and spins the bottle to determine who's next.

NOTES: ▶

The right to pass should be respected during this activity.

MATERIALS: ▶

Pop bottle, deck of feelings cards.

22
Feelings Card Game

GOALS: ▶
- Increase awareness of feelings
- Develop communication skills

DESCRIPTION: ▶

Students select feelings cards represent their personality.

DIRECTIONS: ▶

This game uses the cards that come in the **Stamp Game** kit (see Resources section). Lay out the feelings cards in stacks in the center of the group circle. Call on group members to explain each of the eight feelings listed on the cards. Now ask students to take any number of cards from the piles to demonstrate the feelings they have inside. For example, a student might have a large pile of angry cards, a few guilt cards and one fear card. After everyone has had time to build their stack of cards, ask the group to discuss their stack of cards with the group by explaining why, for example, they have so many angry cards and what the fear cards are for. Additional game variations are provided in the **Stamp Game** kit.

NOTES: ▶

It is also possible to make your own set of feelings cards by cutting out cards from various colors of stiff paper and writing feelings words on them. You may wish to make this a group project.

MATERIALS: ▶

Stamp Game kit.

23
What Should I Do with My Feelings?

Stage: 3

Challenge: LOW

Grades: ALL

GOALS: ▶
- Explore different ways to cope with feelings
- Increase awareness of the variety of feelings

DESCRIPTION: ▶ Group members identify feelings that they struggle with. The group then discusses different strategies to manage these feelings.

DIRECTIONS: ▶ Ask each group member to think of a particular feeling that he or she finds difficult to handle. Ask them to write this feeling on a slip of paper, along with a personal example. Collect these papers, mix them up, draw a slip from the pile, and read it aloud. Ask everyone in turn to explain how they deal with this particular feeling, giving examples from their personal lives. After all have shared, read the next slip of paper and continue the activity in likewise fashion.

NOTES: ▶ Don't be afraid to point out additional methods for dealing with feelings if the group fails to mention strategies you think are important.

MATERIALS: ▶ Slips of paper.

24
Paper Bag People

GOALS: ▶
- Increase awareness of defenses
- Discuss defenses group members use
- Understand appropriate use of defenses

DESCRIPTION: ▶

Group members demonstrate the difference between their public and private lives with the use of paper bag puppets.

DIRECTIONS: ▶

Hand out small paper bags and have crayons, markers, scraps of yarn, and colored construction paper available so group members can make puppet figures that represent themselves.

When they've finished, ask them to think for a minute about how they present themselves to people around them—which feelings are openly shared, which moods, facial expressions, and attitudes they typically present. Ask them to write this information on the outside of their puppet, where it is plainly visible.

Then ask the group to reflect a minute on the many secret thoughts and feelings that they carry around inside of them. These should be written on small slips of paper and placed inside their puppets.

Now that the students have a self-portrait demonstrating both inner and outer thoughts and feelings, the differences can be more easily discussed. Ask students to explain their outside self—how they present themselves to the world around them—and then reach inside their bag and share some of their inside, protected thoughts and feelings. You may wish to ask them if there are any feelings inside their bags they wish were on the outsides of their bags.

Be sure to point out to the group that it's okay to have a private life. No one shares everything about herself with everyone else. Discuss with the group examples of thoughts and feelings that are better off kept to yourself or shared with only the closest of friends. Also ask the group to think of specific feelings or problems that should be shared with others. For example, the group might decide that it's okay to keep feelings of jealousy to yourself but when you're feeling lonely you should reach out to a friend and talk about it.

NOTES: ▶

Let group members know that they don't have to reveal the inner feelings content of their puppets to anyone, so they should feel free to write very personal and private thoughts there.

MATERIALS: ▶

Lunch-sized paper bags, markers, crayons, yarn, construction paper scraps, glue, and slips of paper.

25
Feelings Charades

GOALS: ▶

- Increase awareness of variety of feelings
- Expand feelings vocabulary

DESCRIPTION: ▶

Group members play the game of charades using a feelings word instead of the usual book, movie, or song title.

DIRECTIONS: ▶

Divide students into two equal teams. Ask each team to write ten feelings on separate slips of paper. One member is selected from the guessing team (the team should rotate this position among their members) to act out the feeling word for the rest of his or her team. This student takes a slip of paper from the other team's pile and then acts out this feeling, without speaking, for his or her teammates. The group leader keeps track of how much time elapses before the guessing team correctly identifies the feeling. The two teams alternate until all ten clues have been used. Then the group leader adds up the total time for each team. If you wish to designate a winner, it would be the team with the least time.

NOTES: ▶

Younger students might have a difficult time writing down ten different feelings. In this case, the group leader can either give the students a list of feeling words to choose from, or forgo the slips of paper altogether and simply whisper the feeling word to the student who will be acting out the feeling.

MATERIALS: ▶

Clock or watch with a second hand, blank slips of paper, list of feeling words (see Appendix A).

26
Dealing with Feelings

Stage: 3

Challenge: LOW

Grades: ALL

GOALS: ▶
- Learn how to manage uncomfortable feelings
- Evaluate different coping styles

DESCRIPTION: ▶
Group members identify and evaluate different strategies for coping with uncomfortable feelings.

DIRECTIONS: ▶
First ask the group to make a list on the blackboard of a variety of feelings that can be difficult to deal with, such as anger, fear, jealousy, loneliness. This list doesn't need to be all-inclusive—five to ten feelings are sufficient. Leave an area of blank space between each feeling word.

Once finished, ask the group to discuss different ways to deal with each feeling. Insist that group members offer examples when they suggest a coping strategy. At this point, they shouldn't assess whether the strategy is positive or not—just list a variety of ways to deal with the feeling in question. For example, for feelings of anger group members might suggest screaming, walking away, going for a long run, confronting the person you're angry with, or getting drunk as different ways to cope.

After they've listed these different strategies on the board underneath the feeling, ask them to draw a line through those coping strategies that might feel good in the short run but won't help or may even make the situation worse in the long run. Getting drunk, for example, might temporarily relieve the anger. The morning after, however, the student not only must deal with the anger but he might also have new uncomfortable feelings because of his drinking the previous night. After they have crossed out those coping strategies that are counterproductive, they can move on to the next feeling word.

Once the evaluations are finished, use the remaining group time to reinforce the learning. Ask group members to review the list on the board. If a student admits that she doesn't handle a particular feeling very well, ask her to choose one of the coping strategies from the list that she would be willing to try next time she experiences that feeling.

MATERIALS:
None required.

Section C:
Self-exploration Activities

If there is a single question that makes most of us uneasy, it is: "Who am I?" Most children from chemically dependent families don't have the slightest idea who they are, what they want, what they need, where they are going. Their lives consist primarily of reacting to "the problem."

But in a small group setting they are learning a different way. Instead of focusing on the chemical dependence, support groups are teaching them how to take care of themselves and recover from this seemingly unsolvable problem. Recovery implies direction, and these students must begin to develop a sense of who they are and what they need as they begin this movement to a better place. The activities in this section will help students develop these awarenesses.

27
From Now On

GOALS:

- Encourage goal setting
- Support personal changes made by group members

DESCRIPTION: ▶

Group members review lessons they have learned about themselves during the course of group and identify new behaviors they will continue to practice.

DIRECTIONS: ▶

Review previous sessions of group for the students, pointing out various lessons that have been presented. These examples might include learning that it's important to talk about your feelings, learning how to say "no", learning that we all need to take care of ourselves. After reviewing these past lessons, ask them to reflect on the personal lessons they have learned during group. Then hand out the **From Now On** worksheet (see following page). When they have finished, spend the remaining group time sharing their answers.

NOTES: ▶

If there is an important personal lesson that you think a group member failed to remember and record on her worksheet, bring it to her attention. For example: "What about last week, Cindy, when you realized you never have any time to spend alone. Is that something that should be included on your list of things to do from now on?"

After meeting with these students for a number of sessions, you probably will have specific concerns about some members of the support group. For example, you might notice that Danny often talks about how he gets upset when his parents are arguing, or that Betsy spends a lot of time worrying about how much her mother is drinking. If these students do not address these issues on their worksheets, you can bring it to their attention.

MATERIALS: ▶

From Now On worksheet.

From Now On

On this worksheet list the things that you will do differently based on what you have learned in your support group.

From now on, I'm going to	Instead of
From now on, I'm going to	Instead of
From now on, I'm going to	Instead of
From now on, I'm going to	Instead of
From now on, I'm going to	Instead of

28
How I Want to Be When I Grow Up

Stage: 3

Challenge: LOW

Grades: 9-12

GOALS:

- Encourage students to set personal goals
- Draw attention to the importance of emotional health

DESCRIPTION:

Students describe what kind of people—happy, confident, mature, sensitive—they want to be ten years from now and then discuss what steps need to be taken to ensure this will happen.

DIRECTIONS:

Point out to the group that so often when the future is discussed, we all think in terms of where we want to live or what we want to be doing—"What do you want to be when you grow up?" This activity focuses, instead on how you want to be when you grow up. Do you want to be someone that others turn to for help? Someone that little children like? Do you want to be quiet and thoughtful or the life of the party? Do you want to still be upset about your parent's drinking problem or be able to let go of it and not worry about it?

Ask students to fill out the worksheet (see following page). When everyone is finished, ask them to share their answers with the group. After they have shared both the Now and Future categories, ask group members to describe what is different between the first and second category. Once a student has identified what needs changing (she wants to be more outgoing in the future, for example), ask her what needs to happen for this change to take place. If she isn't able to think of a plan, ask the group for suggestions. For example, a student might, in the future, like to be the kind of person who spends time thinking about what he needs and taking care of himself, and now he sees himself as always worrying about everybody else. The group might suggest to him that every day he do at least one thing for himself rather than going straight home to check whether his Dad has been getting high again.

NOTES:

If students don't offer advice, and look to you for suggestions, resist. Instead, ask another group member what she thinks this student should do to make these changes.

MATERIALS:

How I Want to Be When I Grow Up worksheet.

How I Want to Be When I Grow Up

Below, list eight examples that describe the kind of person you are now (not what you do, but *who* you are and what you are like). Examples could include I'm outgoing, I worry about things too much, I solve everyone's problems, I love to laugh, I'm a good listener.

1) _____

2) _____

3) _____

4) _____

5) _____

6) _____

7) _____

8) _____

Now think about the kind of person you'd like to be ten years from now. Do you want to reduce your shyness and be more outgoing? Do you no longer want to worry so much about what other people think about you? Go ahead and dream. List eight qualities you would like to have be a part of you ten years from now:

1) _____

2) _____

3) _____

4) _____

5) _____

6) _____

7) _____

8) _____

29
Goals and Decisions

GOALS:

- Reinforce personal decisions made by students
- Encourage goal setting
- Identify personal needs and issues

DESCRIPTION: ▶

Group members are asked to identify and set personal goals for themselves and share them with the rest of the group.

DIRECTIONS: ▶

Ask group members to think about the personal issues and problems they have identified as a result of participating in their support group. Pass out sheets of paper and ask them to write these personal issues in the form of a goal that they can work towards. Typical examples include not worrying about a parent's drinking, talking more about feelings with friends, or learning more about how the chemical dependence in their family has affected them.

Also ask group members to write any personal decisions they have made for themselves, such as not drinking or using any other drugs, or attending Alateen regularly.

After everyone has had time to write down their goals and decisions, ask group members to share their answers with the rest of the group. Encourage the rest of the group to give feedback to a student after she has finished sharing her goals and decisions. For example, the group might remind a student about when she told the group she needs to go running if she knows her dad's been drinking. Then she can add this additional goal to her list.

NOTES: ▶

This activity can be used either in the early stages of group or later on, after students are more aware of the affects of chemical dependence on their lives. Using this activity during the initial sessions of group is beneficial in that these clarified goals will provide a sense of direction for the group. You might find, though, that students won't be able to identify personal issues or goals at this early stage. In this case, it will be better to save this activity for when the students' chemical dependence awareness level has been raised. Or, use this activity twice and compare the goals. Group members might find their personal goals to be quite different the second time around.

MATERIALS:

None required.

30
Setting Goals

GOALS: ▶
- Encourage goal setting
- Teach problem-solving skills

DESCRIPTION: ▶
Group members complete a worksheet that helps them clarify and work towards a personal goal.

DIRECTIONS: ▶
Begin this session by asking group members to choose a personal problem they are experiencing, such as fighting with parents or worrying too much about the future, that they would like to change. After everyone has shared their problem with the rest of the group, hand out the **Setting Goals** worksheet (see following page) and ask them to complete it. You may wish to go over it with the group beforehand to make sure they understand the worksheet.

After everyone has finished, ask them to share their work with the group. Don't hesitate to offer suggestions if a group member chooses a goal that is unobtainable or outlines what he won't do rather than what he will do, for example.

Ask all group members to keep their worksheets so they can refer to them as they work towards their goals. Record these personal goals for your own reference. During the next session of group, students can discuss their progress in reaching their goals.

NOTES: ▶
Instead of a one-week review, you may wish to wait several weeks, or follow up on students' progress with a brief discussion several times during the course of the group.

MATERIALS: ▶
Setting Goals worksheet.

Setting Goals

1. A problem I have:

2. What I want to change about this problem:

3. What I can do to help make this change happen:
   1-

   2-

   3-

4. The pros and cons of each of these possibilities are:

   1 **Pros**   **Cons**

   2 **Pros**   **Cons**

   3 **Pros**   **Cons**

5. What I am **willing** to do to help bring about this change:

6. I am willing to do this by this date:

31
What's Different Now?

GOALS: ▶
- Evaluate personal growth
- Reinforce positive changes in group members

DESCRIPTION: ▶ Group members compare their lives from when they began group to how things are going now.

DIRECTIONS: ▶ Discuss with the group how over the course of the group experience they have learned things about themselves and made some changes in their thinking and behaviors. Ask students to share how they first felt when they joined the group. "I felt confused and really angry at my dad," "I didn't see how this group was going to help me," or "I was scared who I'd meet here" are typical answers. When someone has finished sharing, ask the rest of the group what they observed about this particular group member. They might report, "She was really shy" or "Since he never talked about his Dad's drinking problem, I wondered what he was doing here."

Now that everyone has been reminded of how things were when they first joined the group, ask them to draw a timeline on a sheet of paper. One end represents when they first started group and the other end represents the present. Ask group members to record (in chronological order if possible) any changes, insights, backslides, or memorable experiences in their own emotional lives between these two points on the timeline.

Use the remainder of the session to discuss the timelines with the rest of the group.

NOTES: ▶ If long sheets of paper are used, the group could add entries to their timelines as the group progresses. You might want to hand out the timelines occasionally, or tape them to the group room wall so that students can update the timelines whenever they wish.

MATERIALS: ▶ Paper and markers.

32
Johari Window

GOALS: ▶
- Increase awareness of communication patterns
- Reinforce appropriate levels of communication

DESCRIPTION: ▶
After group leaders give a short lecture on the different levels of communication, students identify which levels of communication they use with various people in their lives.

DIRECTIONS: ▶
Using a blackboard, draw and explain a Johari window to the group (see following page for information). Ask group members to give examples of communication for each of the four windows to make sure it is understood. Then pass out sheets of paper and ask them to draw a large Johari window and put several personal communication examples in squares 1 and 2. Point out to them, if necessary, why they can't complete squares 3 and 4. When everyone is finished, ask them to share their windows. After a student has shared what she wrote in squares 1 and 2, ask the rest of the group to offer information for this student to record in square 3.

NOTES: ▶
When group members are offering information to put in the third window for a student, make sure that the group is being gentle. Sometimes group members, though not intending harm, can offer unkind information about another group member's "blind" window.

MATERIALS: ▶
Paper.

For Your Information . . .

Johari Window

I know

1. OPEN	2. PRIVATE
3. BLIND	4. UNKNOWN

You know

Johari window is a convenient model for both understanding and explaining communication dynamics between human beings. And this communication refers to much more than language. Body language, clothing styles, sounds, and degree of eye contact also convey much of the information that is exchanged during the communication process.

The first window is open. It includes information that both you and I know, such as hair color, gender, and the like. Depending on the relationship you have with the person you're communicating with, the open window will include other information: your name, what you like to do in your free time, where you live.

The second window contains our secrets, the things that we know about ourselves that other people don't. Things we've done that we're ashamed of, some of our fears and dreams, and some of the feelings we have about our parent's drinking problem all fit in our private window.

The third window contains all the information other people know about us, but that we ourselves don't know, like what we look like when we walk, little gestures we often use when we're speaking, or that we are very quiet. The only way we can learn about our third window is for others to share this information with us. Sometimes this information is difficult to share or hear.

The fourth window contains the information about us that neither we nor anybody else knows about us. Unconscious thoughts and our night dreams are examples of information that belong in our unknown window.

33
Connections Map

Stage: 2-3

Challenge: MODERATE

Grades: ALL

GOALS:

- Assess social relationships
- Encourage students to strengthen relationships
- Explore trust and intimacy issues

DESCRIPTION: ▶

Group members draw a map depicting their social interaction patterns with family and friends, looking at both the quantity and type of intimacy.

DIRECTIONS: ▶

Begin this session by first discussing relationships with the group. Ask them to offer examples of different types of relationships, such as those between a student and teacher, two casual friends, best friends, students dating, or mother and daughter. Challenge the group to describe what it is that's important about relationships. What is it that we need from other people and which types of relationships are most likely to give us what we need?

Pass out large sheets of newsprint and ask group members to write their own names in the center of their papers and draw circles around them. The rest of the paper should be filled with names of friends, boyfriends or girlfriends, family members and any other people who they have regular contact with. The more intimate the contact, the closer the names will be to their own names in the center. Circles can be drawn around these other names also, and lines should connect all the different names back to group members' names in the center of their papers. It can also be helpful to make these connecting lines bold or weak, depending on the degree of intimacy in the relationship. For example, Marianne might have a thick, black line connecting herself with several close friends and a thin line connecting her father back to her own name. After everyone has finished drawing, ask group members to discuss their drawings.

QUESTIONS:

- Which of these relationships are the most helpful to you?
- After seeing other group members' drawings, is there anything that you wish were different about your connections with people?
- Would you like to be closer to people listed on your drawing?
- What can you change in order to become more connected with these people?

MATERIALS:

Large sheets of newsprint.

34
Whole Person Wheel

GOALS:
- Create awareness of personal needs
- Help students understand their personalities

DESCRIPTION: ▶
Students respond to a number of sentence stems that challenge them to think about who they are and what they need.

DIRECTIONS: ▶
Pass out sheets of newsprint and ask group members to write the word "I" in the center and draw a small circle around it. Then they should draw eight equally-spaced lines outward to the edge of the paper from the center, like the spokes of a wheel. Towards the middle, they should write the following words, one in each section: want, am, have, love, hate, fear, wish, and need. Once done, ask group members to spend some time thinking about and then filling in the triangle sections with appropriate endings to the sentence stems. For example, I need . . . people who care about me, love from my family; I wish . . . my dad would quit drinking, Liz would go out with me. Encourage them to fill in as many examples as they can for each section. Reserve some time at the end of the session to share answers within the group.

MATERIALS:
Sheets of newsprint and markers.

35
Life Maps

GOALS:

- Validate personal experiences
- Establish group unity
- Familiarize leaders with students' family histories

DESCRIPTION:

Students draw a time line of their lives that illustrates their past experiences with the chemical dependence in their family.

DIRECTIONS:

Pass out blank sheets of newsprint paper and markers and give the students an entire group session to draw the chronological history of their lives—from when they were born to the present. They should include anything that's significant to them: moving, parent's divorce, Dad coming home drunk and yelling at everyone, first kiss, changing schools, and so on. Undoubtedly, they will want to know how to record this information, so discuss a few examples: linear progression—construct a timeline, placing significant events in chronological order; boxed captions—draw squares and sketch different scenes in each; journal entries—some students won't want to draw, so let them write out the events and their feelings (see page 76 for a sample **Life Map**). Encourage everyone to be creative and make sure they understand the importance of including their own feelings associated with the past events.

The following several sessions of group should be used to share these life maps. Ask two other members of the group to hold the student's life map for the rest of the group to see while he explains the contents. Give each member a reasonable amount of time to discuss their life map with the group. If students are hesitant to share, or if they skip over things, slow them down by asking questions. Typically, group members will want to give only superficial information: "This happened, and then that happened, and then my brother. . . ." This isn't what you want. Instead, ask questions that encourage identifying feelings: "How did you feel inside when your brother did that?" "How did you feel when your Mom left your Dad?" Encourage other group members to ask questions too; this will set the stage for the group to function as a group rather than the leader always asking the questions.

NOTES:

You should cover between two and three life maps each session of group. More than three life maps in one session means you are moving too quickly; instead, ask additional questions and encourage the students to talk in more depth. Less than two means the students are sharing quite a bit, but it also means that you will be dealing with life maps for many weeks to come.

Remember to be gentle when you ask furthering questions about a group member's life map. This activity is designed to help group members begin to connect their feelings with their experiences, not for students to relive painful episodes.

MATERIALS:

Large sheets of newsprint, markers, or crayons.

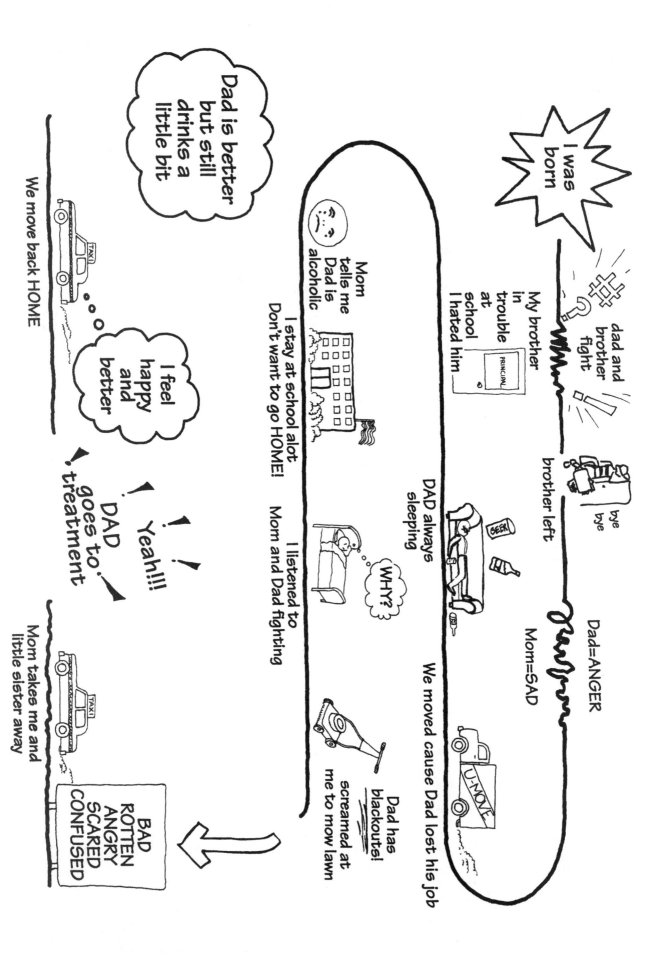

36
Journaling

GOALS: ▶
- Encourage students to reflect on their thoughts and feelings
- Increase self-awareness
- Strengthen writing skills

DESCRIPTION: ▶

Group members are taught how to record their thoughts and feelings in a journal.

DIRECTIONS: ▶

Introduce the concept of journaling to the group by explaining the positive aspects of keeping a journal:

1—It helps you understand your own thoughts and feelings.

2—It provides an avenue for expressing thoughts and feelings that you wouldn't ever share with others.

3—You can read back through previous entries and see how your feelings and problems have changed over time.

Tell the group that each week, the first five minutes of group will be set aside for writing in journals. Make sure the group members understand that they can write whatever they wish, and that nobody will read their journals. They are private. They can keep their journals in the group room or, if they want to write more during the week, they can take the journals with them and bring them back each week.

NOTES:

You may wish to expand on this activity. Here are several different options to consider:

1—After the group has finished writing each week, ask if anybody would like to share what he or she has written.

2—Near the last session of the support group, set aside one session for students to read through their journals and then discuss what has changed during the course of the group sessions as evidenced by their journal entries.

Regardless of how this activity is handled, make sure you show group members that you take their privacy seriously by carefully collecting and putting their journals away in a safe place each week.

MATERIALS:

Spiral notebooks or sheets of lined paper stapled together (one sheet for each session of group).

37
Fantasy Islands

GOALS:
- Clarify personal values
- Identify personally important people and places
- Encourage discussion of present circumstances

DESCRIPTION: ▶

Group members draw their own island country, deciding who and what to include. The islands are discussed when everyone has finished drawing.

DIRECTIONS: ▶

After handing out large sheets of newsprint, tell group members to draw the outline of a large island that will be their own. After they have drawn the island's shape, let them know that, since this is their island, they are in charge of who and what is on the island. And since this is a fantasy island, anything goes: Candy trees, rivers of warm water, a house built out of gold, a remote section of the island for their parents to live, no rules, lots of rules. Encourage them to be creative (see following page for an example). Save some time at the end of the session for group members to discuss their islands.

QUESTIONS: ▶
- Who is welcome on your island?
- What is especially important about your island?
- What aspects of your island are similar to your life now?
- What aspects of your island are different from your life now?
- What does Julie's island tell us about her? (Ask the rest of the group).

NOTES:

If the group seems hesitant or unsure of this task, it's best for you, as the group leader, to just start drawing your own island—soon the others will follow suit.

MATERIALS:

Large sheets of newsprint, markers, and crayons.

FANTASY ISLAND

Sunny Strip (where me and all my friends hang out)

Nobody over 16 allowed

water skiing

Skate board parking place

.2 k to my house

Candy Forest

RULES
1. Everyone gets along
2. No smoking
3. Sunny every day
4. Adults only when invited
5. No talking behind anyone's back
6. No cars!

My house

For my use only

Mystery Mountain

Parent Village

The bike garage

Guest Bungalows

Arrival Pier

38
Draw Your School

Stage: 2-3

Challenge: LOW

Grades: ALL

GOALS:
- Communicate feelings and attitudes about school
- Explore the relationship between school and personal issues

DESCRIPTION:
Group members draw personal impressions of their school, including their classrooms, teachers, and other students.

DIRECTIONS:
Ask group members to close their eyes and imagine their school, classrooms, and the teachers they interact with throughout the day. Ask them to concentrate on their emotional responses to their school day such as how it feels when they are waiting for the bus in the morning, at a pep-fest, in a boring class, spending a few minutes talking with the teacher after class, or standing in the halls while everyone is rushing past.

After they have an emotional picture of their school experience in mind, hand out large sheets of newsprint and ask them to draw their school and the significant people that they interact with there. Point out that their drawings should focus on this emotional picture—they shouldn't try to make their drawings a true physical representation of the school (see following page for an example).

Once everyone has finished, spend the remaining time discussing these drawings.

QUESTIONS:
- What feeling words would you use to describe your school?
- What aspects of school do you like the most? The least?
- Are there adults in the school whom you could talk to if you had a problem? Who are they?
- Has your impression of school changed over the years? Why or why not?
- What can you change to make school a more positive experience for yourself?

MATERIALS:
Newsprint and markers.

MY SCHOOL DRAWING

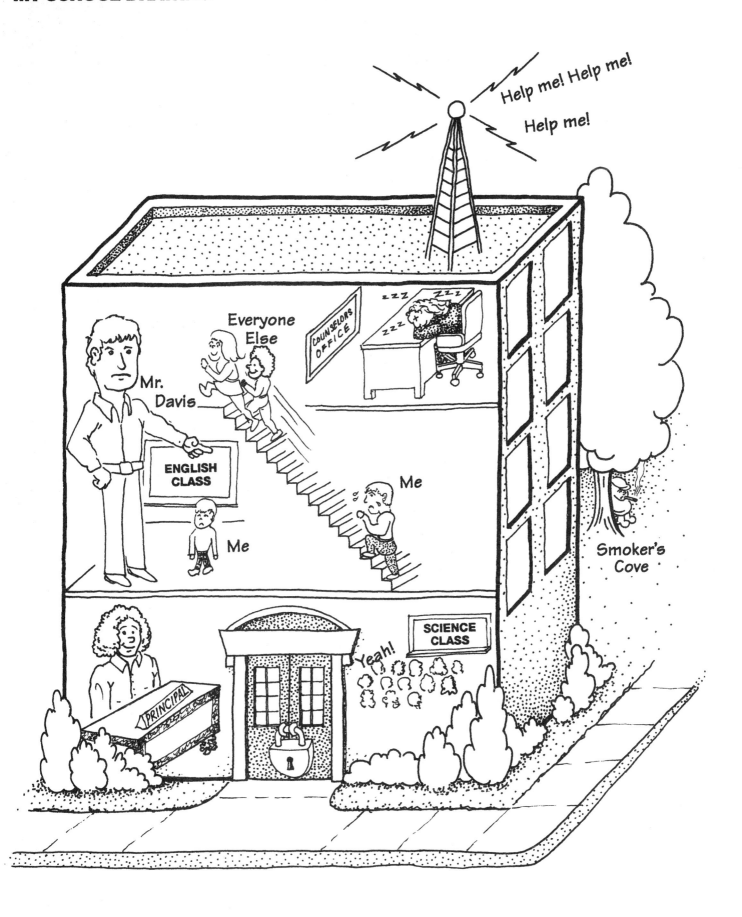

39
Where Do You Stand?

Stage: 2-3
Challenge:
MODERATE
Grades: 9-12

GOALS: ▶
- Affirm personal values
- Create discussion opportunities
- Expose group members to diverse opinions

DESCRIPTION: ▶

Questions are posed to group members who then indicate their personal agreement or disagreement.

DIRECTIONS: ▶

Using masking tape, create a line running the length of the group room. Place an "X" in the center. The right side of the "X" signifies agreement and to the left of the "X" signifies disagreement. Tell the students that you'll read a statement to them that they should first think about and then indicate their own belief by choosing a spot to stand on the tape line. Point out that the farther out they stand from the "X", the stronger they feel about the statement

After you have read a statement (listed on the following page) and all group members are standing somewhere on the line, spend a few minutes asking students to explain or defend their position before reading the next statement. In addition to using the statements provided, you could ask group members to think of additional issues to explore.

NOTES: ▶

Encourage honesty and individuality. When most students are clumped together on the line, give recognition to the sole student who has a different opinion—even if it's a strange one. The focus of this activity isn't to solve these issues or even to reach a consensus; the goal is to get students thinking about what they believe and to explore different points of view.

MATERIALS: ▶

Masking tape and a list of statements.

Where Do You Stand?

1. Alcohol should be illegal for everyone.

2. Treatment centers are successful in helping people quit drinking or using other drugs.

3. The probability of me having a problem with alcohol or other drugs later in life is very low.

4. There are many things I would like to change about myself.

5. My parent with the drinking problem will never quit drinking.

6. Running away can solve some problems.

7. I like spending time at home.

8 Parents are generally good to their children.

9. Adults caught driving under the influence should be put in jail.

10. All in all, I'm a pretty good person who usually does what's right.

11. Alcoholics who drink hard liquor are worse than those who only drink beer.

12. School is a pretty good place to be.

13. Most teachers are fair and care about their students.

14. All chemically dependent people should go to treatment.

15. Chemical dependence is a big problem in our community.

16. Talking about your feelings is very important.

17. You shouldn't let people know when you're angry with them.

18. Everybody should be in a support group.

19. I don't care who knows that I come to this group.

20. Things at home are better now than they were a year ago.

40
Five Great Things About Me

GOALS: ▶
- Increase self-esteem
- Help students identify what makes them feel good about themselves

DESCRIPTION: ▶ Students are asked to make and share a list of five qualities about themselves that increase their self-esteem.

DIRECTIONS: ▶ Ask students to think for a minute about the things that help them feel good about themselves. This can include achievements: "I got straight A's last quarter," "I'm on the starting team for basketball this season"; personal strengths: "I'm a good listener," "my friends can really trust me"; or physical qualities: "I'm a fast runner," "I've got deep brown eyes."

After making sure that everyone understands what self-esteem is, ask them to write down five things about themselves that they feel proud of. When they're finished, ask them to share their lists with the rest of the group. Most group members will focus on things they do rather than inherent qualities such as having a warm smile, nice eyes, or being thoughtful towards others. After everyone has finished sharing their lists, discuss the difference between doing and being. Point out to them that getting self-esteem exclusively from things that you do places conditions on your self-esteem. Self-esteem stemming from knowing you've got a warm personality is permanent; self-esteem from the fastest hundred-yard dash isn't always a sure thing.

Ask group members to review their list and to change every item that was "doing-based" to "feeling-based." Share these new lists in the group.

NOTES: ▶ If a group member can't think of five items for his list, ask the rest of the group to offer some suggestions.

MATERIALS: ▶ Paper.

41
My Song

GOALS: ▶
- Clarify personal values
- Identify personally important people and places
- Encourage discussion of current issues

DESCRIPTION: ▶
Group members bring lyrics of a favorite song to group and, after reading them out loud, discuss why the lyrics are important to them.

DIRECTIONS: ▶
The week previous to this session, ask group members to choose a favorite song and bring the lyrics to group. Tell them they will be asked to explain the song's personal importance.

 The following week ask group members to read the lyrics to their songs out loud and then explain to the group why the song is important.

QUESTIONS: ▶
- Why did you choose this song?
- What do you think this song's message is?
- How does this song make you feel?
- Why is this song important to you?

NOTES: ▶
Be aware of the fact that some students might bring lyrics that contain profane language or lyrics promoting sexism, racism, or other offensive actions. If you feel uncomfortable including these topics in group discussion, you may not want to use this activity. Another option would be to say something like "Choose a favorite song that doesn't contain any objectionable language or content."

MATERIALS: ▶
None required.

42
All About Me Book

GOALS:

- Increase self-awareness
- Provide personal validation and recognition

DESCRIPTION:

Students construct a book of pages filled with items that describe themselves.

DIRECTIONS: ▶

In preparation for this activity, during the week previous to this session ask students to bring a few items describing themselves to group the following week. This can include drawings, pictures, awards, found objects, pictures of a pet—anything they wish. You'll also need to bind ten to fifteen pieces of construction paper together with string or staples into a book for each member of group. You may wish to do this outside of group or have the group members make their own books.

   After explaining to the group that the focus of this activity is to make a book about themselves, encourage group members to put anything in their books that represents their hobbies, interests, dreams, personality, family. They may also wish to draw illustrations, write captions, or decorate the front cover. Use the remaining time of this session to share the books with the rest of the group, explaining the drawings and the significance of pictures and other objects.

NOTES: ▶

Rather than using one large block of time, you may wish to ask group members to complete only one page of their books at a time, collecting the books and passing them out again every other week of group, for example. This way, the finished book is more likely to show the diversity of their personalities. And after numerous short sessions of book work, then the finished books can be shared with the rest of the group. You could also save the books and on the last day of group everyone could sign each other's book, like a yearbook-signing party.

   If group members bring objects that can't be attached to pages of a book, you could give them a small box, such as a shoe box, to decorate and use instead of a book. Another approach would be to simply have them share their objects with the group without making a book.

MATERIALS:

Squares of construction paper, paper hole punch, string, scissors, stapler, transparent tape, glue, markers, crayons, and boxes.

43
This Is Me Collage

GOALS: ▶
- Encourage nonverbal self-expression
- Help students become more aware of their own personalities

DESCRIPTION: ▶ Using magazine pictures and words, students make a collage that expresses their personalities.

DIRECTIONS: ▶ After making sure that group members understand the term personality, ask them to describe how personalities can differ, such as quiet, moody, outgoing, or angry. Point out that, even though we might use one word to describe someone's personality, we all really have very complex collections of feelings, thoughts, attitudes, and beliefs. A student who is quiet at school might be loud and bossy at home, for example.

Ask group members to flip through magazines you've provided, looking for pictures and words that are descriptive of their own personalities. Ask them to glue the pictures and words onto a sheet of construction paper as they page through the magazines. Reserve enough time at the end of the session for students to share their collages with the rest of the group. If they are hesitant to explain their collages, you could ask them specific questions about pictures or words they included.

NOTES: ▶ As group members share their collages, look for central themes such as reoccurring images of anger, expressed love, or even simply the fact that a group member has many pictures of food. Either point these themes out to them as they take their turns sharing or, better yet, ask the rest of the group if they notice a central theme in a group member's collage.

MATERIALS: ▶ Variety of magazines representing cultural diversity (check with art classes, school library, or used book stores), scissors, glue, sturdy sheets of construction paper.

44
Three Symbols of Me

GOALS: ▶

- Increase self-awareness
- Encourage self-expression
- Increase group unity

DESCRIPTION: ▶

Group members bring three objects that are symbolic of themselves to share with the rest of the group.

DIRECTIONS: ▶

During the group session before this activity, ask everyone to bring three objects to the next session of group that are representative of themselves—their dreams, feelings, goals, experiences. Students typically will bring objects such as pictures, a radio, or things they have made.

   During this session ask group members to share their objects with the group, explaining why they are symbolic and why they chose them.

QUESTIONS: ▶

- Why is this object important to you?
- Is there a story behind this object?
- Is there something that you wanted to bring but couldn't?

NOTES: ▶

Some group members might want to bring a pet, so decide how you want to handle this issue before introducing the activity. Also, if a group member forgets his objects let him describe his symbolic object to the rest of the group.

MATERIALS: ▶

None required.

45
My Bill of Rights

Stage: 2-3

Challenge: LOW

Grades: ALL

GOALS: ▶
- Encourage students to respect themselves
- Introduce the concept of personal boundaries
- Help students to assert themselves

DESCRIPTION: ▶

After discussing personal rights and their importance, group members create a list of rights for themselves and then share them with the group.

DIRECTIONS: ▶

First discuss personal rights with the group. Ask them for examples of rights that we all should have, such as the right to express our thoughts and feelings, the right to privacy, the right to safety. After this concept is understood by all and examples have been given, ask the students to draw up their own list of personal rights. This list will reflect what rights are important to them. When finished, ask group members to share their list with the rest of the group.

QUESTIONS: ▶
- Which of your personal rights are respected by others?
- Which of your personal rights are violated? By whom?
- What can you do to ensure your rights are respected?

MATERIALS: ▶

Paper.

46
Tape Your Space

GOALS: ▶
- Develop understanding of personal boundaries
- Explore personal space needs

DESCRIPTION: ▶
Group members use masking tape to represent their personal space boundaries.

DIRECTIONS: ▶
First discuss the topic of personal space with the group by pointing out the fact that some people like to keep a lot of distance, while others enjoy body contact. Ask group members to imagine how they would feel if, while waiting in a bus station, someone came and sat down right next to them on an otherwise empty bench. Point out how, though at the beginning of a group session all chairs are in a tight circle, by the end of the session students have unconsciously spread their chairs farther apart.

Next, pass out rolls of masking tape and ask students to tape off boundaries on the floor representing their own personal space. Some students might tape off only a tight square, while others might want an entire corner of the group room. After they are finished, ask each group member to explain his own personal space needs.

QUESTIONS: ▶
- Why did you take such a little (or large) area?
- Do you think you need more or less space than most people?
- Explain how people invade your space.
- How do you feel when people intrude in your space?

NOTES: ▶
It's important that everyone start taping their boundaries at the same time so that aggressive group members aren't allowed to tape off all available space! For this reason, give group members their own roll of masking tape.

MATERIALS: ▶
Rolls of masking tape for every member of your group.

47
My Own Needs

GOALS: ▶
- Identify personal needs
- Evaluate how well students' needs are met

DESCRIPTION:
Group members discuss the concept of physical and emotional needs and use a worksheet to identify their own needs and how well these needs are being met

DIRECTIONS: ▶
First ask the group to make a list of what our physical needs include, such as food, shelter, clothing. Then ask them to discuss what humans need in order to be emotionally healthy. These needs can include being loved, feeling appreciated, being safe, having time alone. Remind them that not everyone has the same needs. You might want to record this list on the blackboard as group members identify various needs.

After they finish this list, have them complete the **My Own Needs** worksheet (see following page), which asks them to identify their own personal needs and rate how successful they are at getting their needs met. Use the remaining time to discuss the results.

MATERIALS: ▶
My Own Needs worksheet.

My Own Needs

Everyone has emotional needs—what are yours? Think about this for a moment and then write down six of your own needs below. After you have finished your list, complete the right-hand side of the worksheet. Next to each of the emotional needs you identified, rate how well this need is met by placing an "X" on the line.

My Emotional Needs Are:	Not met		Met
1: _____	1_____	5 _____	10
2: _____	1_____	5 _____	10
3: _____	1_____	5 _____	10
4: _____	1_____	5 _____	10
5: _____	1_____	5 _____	10
6: _____	1_____	5 _____	10

Section D: Chemical Dependence Information Activities

There is perhaps no other disease that includes as much shame, confusion, and denial as does chemical dependence. Giving young people accurate information concerning alcohol and other drugs is an important way to help them understand the nature and characteristics of the disease.

Support groups are a wonderful opportunity to teach students what chemical dependence is all about. Students need to understand that their parents have a disease and that, just as if it were diabetes or cancer, the young people didn't cause it, aren't to blame, and there isn't anything they can do to fix it—not better grades, not throwing the booze out, not telling funnier jokes.

Young people need to learn about blackouts, addiction, enabling, denial, relapse, and recovery. After all, as a family member of a person with chemical dependence, they're affected by these issues and most likely left frustrated and confused. When they begin to understand the dynamics and symptoms of this disease, they are much more able to put the problem in its true perspective and work on taking care of themselves.

48
The Disease Called Chemical Dependence

Stage: 3

Challenge: HIGH

Grades: 9-12

GOALS:

- Provide information about chemical dependence
- Help students separate the disease from the person

DESCRIPTION:

The group uses a set of cards, each with a chemical dependence term on one side, to explore different aspects of chemical dependence and how it affects members of the students' families.

DIRECTIONS:

Prepare a set of cards by writing key chemical dependence terms (see following page) on 3 x 5 inch index cards. Place the cards face down in the center of the group so that group members can take turns drawing. When a student draws a card, he should first explain the concept to the rest of the group (if he isn't familiar with the term, he can ask the rest of the group for help), and then connect this particular concept to his family. For example, if the key term was denial, a group member might explain how everyone in her family knows that her mom has a drinking problem, but her Mom refuses to admit that there's anything wrong and insists that she isn't an alcoholic.

NOTES:

If the game is proceeding rather quickly, you could instruct the person who drew a card to call on other group members to also give personal examples of the key term.

MATERIALS:

Chemical dependence term cards.

Chemical Dependence Terms

Here is a list of terms to include on the cards:

ACOA
adult child of an alcoholic

AFTERCARE
a chemical dependence program that follows after treatment

AL-ANON
a self-help group for adults affected by someone else's chemical dependence

ALATEEN
a self-help group for teenagers affected by someone else's chemical dependence

ALCOHOLICS ANONYMOUS
a self-help group for people with a drinking problem

BIG BOOK
the basic text for Alcoholics Anonymous

BLACKOUTS
temporary alcohol-induced memory loss

CHEMICAL DEPENDENCE
a relationship with mind-altering chemicals that causes problems

CLEAN AND SOBER
abstaining from drugs, including alcohol

CODEPENDENT
a harmful relationship with a chemically dependent person

CONFRONTING
presenting reality

CONGRUENT
acting in a way that is consistent with how you're feeling

CONTROLLING
attempting to make things happen in a certain way

DEFENSES
behaviors we use to protect or hide our feelings

DELIRIUM TREMENS
sweats, anxiety, and hallucinations associated with withdrawal symptoms
of alcohol addiction

DELUSION a false, persistent belief

DENIAL refusing to see the drinking or other drug problem

DETACHMENT emotional separation from a chemically dependent
person's behavior

DRY DRUNK
recovering, sober people acting as if they were still drinking

DYSFUNCTIONAL
non-productive attitudes, feelings, and behavior

ENABLING
allowing or encouraging someone's self-destructive behavior to continue

FAMILY DISEASE
describes the fact that entire families are affected by one member's chemical dependence

HALFWAY HOUSE
a structured, independent living facility for recovering chemically dependent people

INTERVENTION
a process in which persons close to a chemically dependent person lovingly but firmly help that person face the reality of his or her chemical dependence

LETTING GO
emotionally separating from a chemically dependent person's behavior

LEVELING
letting others know how I feel in an open, honest manner

NARCOTICS ANONYMOUS
a self-help program for people whose chemical dependence was mostly on drugs other than alcohol

NURTURING
being supportive and caring

RECOVERY
the process of recovering from chemical dependence

RECOVERY PROGRAM
all the things a chemically dependent person does to maintain sobriety

RELAPSE
the process of returning back to chemical use

REVERSE TOLERANCE
a person achieving a certain level of intoxication with progressively smaller amounts of the chemical

TOLERANCE
a person needing to use progressively larger amounts of a chemical to achieve a certain level of intoxication

TREATMENT
an intensive program to help a chemically dependent person achieve continual abstinence and recovery

TWELVE STEPS
guidelines for members of a twelve-step, self-help program such as Alcoholics Anonymous or Al-Anon

49
Four Phases of Chemical Dependence

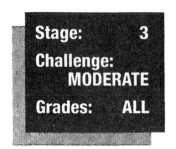

Stage: 3
Challenge:
      MODERATE
Grades: ALL

GOALS:

- Create an awareness of the different phases of chemical dependence
- Help students to see chemical dependence as a disease

DESCRIPTION: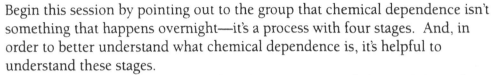

Using a short lecture combined with demonstration and discussion, the leader illustrates the basic concepts of the four phases of chemical dependence.

DIRECTIONS:

Begin this session by pointing out to the group that chemical dependence isn't something that happens overnight—it's a process with four stages. And, in order to better understand what chemical dependence is, it's helpful to understand these stages.

First ask group members to explain the progression of chemical dependence in their own words. Once the group has struggled with this briefly, come to their rescue with a short presentation using the information on the following page. In order to make this information more meaningful, use the group to demonstrate the four stages as you explain them. Begin by asking two students to sit in the center of the group circle. These two students will represent chemicals (let them choose which chemical). Also choose one student to become chemically dependent. The remaining circle of students will represent life.

As you explain the first phase (learning), ask the chemically dependent student to enter the circle and briefly join the two students representing chemicals. He should make a return visit to the chemicals as you explain the second stage (seeking). During the explanation of the third stage (loss of choice), he should return to the chemicals again, but the students representing the chemicals should grab him tight and only let him go after he promises to return later. Then, during the explanation of the fourth and final stage (using to feel normal), he should be grabbed by the chemicals and not let go. To make even more of a visual impact, the students could pin him to the floor.

After the demonstration is finished, use the remaining time to discuss the chemical dependence in group members' families.

QUESTIONS:

- In which stage do you think your chemically dependent family member might be?
- Are there other members of your family that you're concerned about? Why?
- What stage do you think they might be in?

CONTINUED ON NEXT PAGE

NOTES:

In order to make the demonstration more effective, you might consider taking the two group members who will be representing the chemicals aside and explain their roles to them privately, rather than in front of the rest of the group. When using the discussion questions, be sure to point out that there isn't any way they can know for sure which stage their family member is in—you're simply asking their opinions.

Also, be sure to mention that many people do recover from chemical dependence. Many people who were in the fourth stage are now leading happy, sober lives.

MATERIALS: ▶

None required.

For Your Information . . .

The Four Phases of Chemical Dependence

LEARNING:

As people first use a chemical, such as alcohol, they learn that this chemical changes how they are feeling, usually in a positive way. This is a pleasant experience for most people. Once the effects of the chemical wear off, these people return to how they were feeling before they used the chemical.

SEEKING:

After several experiences with the chemical, people move out of the learning stage and into the seeking stage. A person in this stage knows what alcohol will do and she knows how much she needs to drink in order to achieve this certain affect. Unfortunately, some people in stage two use mind-altering chemicals to get rid of uncomfortable feelings, such as anger or loneliness. Using chemicals is a temporary solution, however, because the painful feelings return—unsolved—when the effects of the chemical wear off.

LOSS OF CHOICE:

Some people move from the second stage into the third stage. This stage signals the presence of chemical dependence. People in this stage have lost the ability to choose whether to use chemicals or not. Up until this stage a person could choose from many different ways to deal with his feelings, but now he relies on only one way—the use of chemicals. Whenever he is feeling bad, he turns to the chemicals for relief. The chemicals are now in control. We still don't totally understand why some people move from the second to the third stage and other people stay in the first or second stage.

USING TO FEEL NORMAL:

This last stage is characterized by deterioration in all areas of life—personal relationships, work, and health. A person in this stage is always feeling bad and uses chemicals in an attempt just to feel normal once again. When a person reaches this stage, most everyone recognizes that there is a problem. It would be hard not to.

NOTE:

These four stages describe the process chemically dependent people go through. Keep in mind, though, that most people experience the first two stages described here. This doesn't necessarily imply they're on their way to becoming chemically dependent.

50
Chemical Dependence Crosswords

Stage: 2-3

Challenge: LOW

Grades: ALL

GOALS: ▶

- Increase students' chemical dependence vocabulary
- Encourage teamwork and group unity

DESCRIPTION: ▶

Opposing teams work to complete a crossword puzzle composed of chemical dependence terms.

DIRECTIONS: ▶

Split the support group into equal teams. Ask each team to choose a captain. The captain is responsible for communicating the team's answers and question choices to the leader. The support group leader shouldn't accept any answers from team members other than the team captain. Draw the empty frame of the puzzle on the blackboard and choose which team will go first. Each team gets thirty seconds for their turn regardless of how many blanks they fill. When it is a team's turn they choose a horizontal or vertical blank line. The leader then reads the clue for this blank out loud. The team should discuss possible answers among themselves before the team captain offers the answer to the leader. If the team is correct, it receives one point and may continue with a new clue, providing there still is time remaining on the thirty-second clock. The support group leader should write correct definitions in the puzzle squares as they are identified. If their answer is incorrect, they must move on to a new crossword clue (they can return to this clue next turn if they wish). When thirty seconds have passed, their turn is over and the next team begins. The game continues until all clues have been filled.

NOTES: ▶

Two crossword puzzles representing different levels of difficulty are provided (see following page) so that you may pick a puzzle with age-appropriate vocabulary. Puzzle A is for junior high school students and puzzle B is for senior high school students.

If you require additional puzzles, either design them yourself or, if you have at least two different support groups, ask the groups to design and then swap puzzles.

MATERIALS: ▶

Crossword puzzles, thirty-second timer or clock, blackboard.

Puzzle A
ACROSS 3) defenses 4) blackout 8) pills 10) feelings 11) bottles 12) Alateen 14) anger 15) listen 17) sad 20) abuse 21) adults. **DOWN** 1) help 2) alcoholic 3) drugs 5) chemicals 6) treatment 7) disease 9) steps 13) talk 16) stress 18) drunk 19) group

Puzzle B
ACROSS 2) chemical 3) ACOA 6) defenses 7) narcotics 8) book 11) control 12) Step 14) treatment 16) anger 18) enable 19) Alateen 21) relapse 23) nurturing 24) Twelve 25) dry drunk 26) blackout **DOWN** 1) halfway 2) CA 4) addiction 5) recovering 6) dysfunctional 9) Anonymous 10) confront 11) codependence 13) aftercare 15) tolerance 17) intervention 20) family 22) drunk 23) new

Crossword Puzzle A

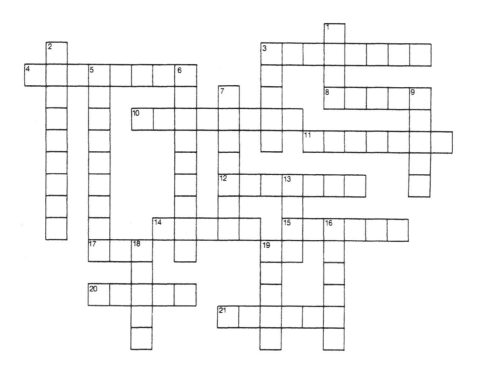

ACROSS

3 We protect ourselves with these
4 Alcohol-induced memory loss
8 Sleeping _____
10 It's important to talk about these
11 Sometimes we want to throw these out
12 Where young people can get help
14 Rage
15 How friends can help
17 Feeling blue
20 Physical or verbal
21 When in danger, reach out to _____

DOWN

1 A cry for _____
2 Addicted to C2H5OH
3 Substances that can change your feelings
5 Pills, marijuana, alcohol
6 Where alcoholics and addicts go for help
7 Alcoholism is a _____
9 The Twelve _____
13 The secret for feeling better
16 Tension and anxiety
18 Intoxicated
19 Support _____

Crossword Puzzle B

ACROSS

2 _____ dependence
3 Adults who have an alcoholic parent
6 Used to protect ourselves
7 Heroin, opium
8 The Big _____ of Alcoholics Anonymous
11 A symptom of drinking problems is lack of ____
12 The First _____
14 Where chemically dependent people go for help
16 Rage
18 Allow the problem to continue
19 Al-Anon for young people
21 Return to using chemicals
23 Supporting and encouraging
24 _____ Steps
25 Not recovering but not drinking (2 words)
26 Alcohol-induced memory loss

DOWN

1 _____ house
2 Cocaine Anonymous
4 Can be physical or psychological
5 Clean and sober
6 Not working well
9 Alcoholics _____
10 Present reality
11 The illness of family members
13 After treatment
15 Need more chemicals because of increased _____
17 Formal group confrontation
20 _____disease
22 Intoxicated
23 Sobriety provides a _____ outlook

51
Research Report

GOALS:

- Increase understanding of chemical dependence
- Eliminate common misconceptions about chemical dependence

DESCRIPTION:

Students are each assigned a topic word to research. The following week of group each student gives a small report to the group about what she has learned.

DIRECTIONS:

From the list of vocabulary words (see following page), ask each student to select a term. Ask them to research this word in the library or to use other resources such as a discussion with a recovering person or counselor. The following week of group, ask each student to spend a few minutes explaining this key term to the rest of the group. If they are able, ask the group member to relate a personal example that connects this term to her personal life. For example, if the term were "blackouts", the student could explain what blackouts are and then also describe a time that her father had a blackout and how confusing it was for her because it seemed like her father was losing his mind. Encourage the rest of the group to ask questions of the person who is explaining the term.

MATERIALS:

None required.

Chemical Dependence Terms

Aftercare
Al-Anon
Alateen
Alcoholics Anonymous
Big Book
Blackouts
Chemical dependence
Codependence
Congruence
Defenses
Delirium Tremens
Delusion
Denial
Detach
Disengage
Dry drunk
Dysfunctional
Enabling
Family disease
Halfway house
Hitting bottom
Intervention
Letting Go
Leveling
Narcotics Anonymous
Nurturing
Physical addiction
Psychological addiction
Rationalize
Recovery
Recovery program
Relapse
Reverse tolerance
Therapy
Tolerance
Treatment center
Twelve Steps

NOTE: Refer to activity #48 for definitions of many of these terms.

52
Book Report

GOALS: ▶
- Increase awareness of available media resources
- Learn more about chemical dependence

DESCRIPTION: ▶
Group members choose a book or video from the selection the group leader has brought to group. The following week, students give a small report to the rest of the group.

DIRECTIONS: ▶
Bring a number of print and video resources to group. These resources should include books, workbooks, and videos that are both age and topic appropriate for the group members (see Resources section).

Ask the students to select one book or video, instructing them that they should take this resource with them, read or view it, and then be prepared to give a short report to the rest of the group. These oral reports should be informal, explaining what the student learned from the book or video. Use the next session of group for the students' reports.

QUESTIONS: ▶
- What did you learn by reading the book or watching the video?
- What are three important points that the book or video is making about chemical dependence?
- Would you recommend this book or video to other students? Why or why not?

NOTES: ▶
Some students might hesitate to bring these resources home for fear their parents might be upset when they see the title of the book or video. When this is the case, arrange access after school or during a study hall period.

MATERIALS: ▶
Selection of books, workbooks, pamphlets and videos (see Resources section).

53
The Inheritance

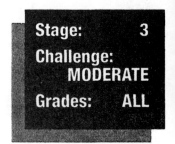

Stage: 3
Challenge: MODERATE
Grades: ALL

GOALS:
- Increase awareness of genetic predisposition to chemical dependence
- Encourage students to abstain from alcohol and other drugs

DESCRIPTION:

Group members are presented information concerning their genetic and environmental predisposition to chemical dependence. This information is presented through a combination of video, lecture, and discussion. Alternative activities to a video are also discussed.

DIRECTIONS:

Use the information on the next page to make a short presentation about the nature of genetic predisposition. Encourage an interactive approach by asking their opinions (for example, what percent of children with chemically dependent parents become chemically dependent themselves?) before you outline the facts. Discussion can stem from a variety of questions: Is chemical dependence passed on genetically, is it learned through modeling parents' drinking behaviors, or does it stem from the fact that these kids often have traumatic childhoods? Can the students identify a history of chemical dependence in their extended families? Do the group members think they're at risk? Why or why not? Do they use mind-altering chemicals now?

You may also want to begin this activity by showing the video *My Father's Son* (see Resources section). After the video, ask group members what they think will happen to the teenager in the video. Does the son have a problem with chemicals? What are the chances he will in the future?

Next, outline some basic facts about genetic predisposition (see information on following page) and begin a discussion in which group members connect this information with their own families. Are there histories of chemical dependence in their families? Do they think that they are at risk for becoming chemically dependent? Why or why not?

NOTES:

The video, while not crucial to this activity, is an excellent vehicle for presenting the concept of genetic predisposition.

MATERIALS:

For Your Information, *My Father's Son* video (optional).

For Your Information . . .

Chemical Dependence — Learned or Inherited?

Much has been written concerning the relationship between parents' chemical dependence and their sons or daughters' chemical use. Everyone agrees that the children of parents who are chemically dependent are at high risk for becoming chemically dependent themselves. What isn't clear is exactly how this relationship is passed on from parent to child.

Genetic Predisposition: This position supports the idea that simply by having a biological parent who is chemically dependent, you are at risk for becoming chemically dependent. There is research demonstrating that children of alcoholics who are adopted into healthy families as infants still show high rates of alcoholism when they have grown up.

Common sense would also support the idea that, since children's primary role models are their parents, these children also become high risk simply by modeling what they see their parents doing—which is, in this case, a lot of drinking or using other drugs. The fact that every time their parent is troubled he or she drinks becomes a powerful, though harmful, lesson.

Environmental: Then there are those who point to the fact that these children grow up in turbulent, painful, and dysfunctional home environments. Simply put, these children have a painful childhood and carry these problems around with them, eventually turning to mind-altering chemicals for escape and relief.

All of this boils down to the classic nature vs. nurture controversy for which there are few simple answers. Currently, the majority believe that the answer is a combination of all three factors, each contributing to the amount of risk. Here are some current statistics:

- More than half of all alcoholics have an alcoholic parent.[1]
- Children of alcoholics are at high risk of developing alcoholism themselves or marrying someone who is or will become alcoholic.[2]
- The single most important predictor of alcoholism for a child is having an alcoholic parent.[3]
- Fifty-eight percent of children with an alcoholic parent will become alcoholic themselves.[4]
- Thirty percent of children with an alcoholic parent will marry an alcoholic.[5]

---

[1] Linda Christensen, *Facts, Feelings, Family and Friends* (Minneapolis: Johnson Institute, 1990).
[2] Ibid.
[3] Nancy Cotton, "The Familial Incidence of Alcoholism: A Review," *Journal of Alcohol Studies* vol. 40, no. 1 (1979): 89-115.
[4] Margaret Hindman, "Children of Alcoholic Parents," *Alcohol, Health and Research World*, (Winter 1975): 2-6
[5] Claudia Black, "Innocent Bystanders at Risk: The Children of Alcoholics," *Alcoholism*, (January/February 1981): 22-26

54
Field Trip to a Treatment Center

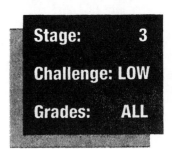

Stage: 3

Challenge: LOW

Grades: ALL

GOALS:

- Challenge misconceptions about treatment centers
- Reinforce concept of chemical dependence as a disease
- Reduce anxiety of students anticipating a family member entering a treatment program

DESCRIPTION:

Support group members spend a few hours visiting a chemical dependence treatment center to become more familiar with a typical program.

DIRECTIONS:

Arrange for a tour of a treatment center in your community. Since this isn't a typical request, make sure that the information and activities will be both interesting and age-appropriate for your group members. Possible activities could include a tour of the building, a mini group session, and a description of how children of patients are involved in the program.

NOTES:

A week or two before the treatment center visit, hand out parent permission slips for group members to take home. If visiting a treatment center is not an option for your group, then invite a treatment center counselor to give a presentation to your group.

MATERIALS:

Parent permission slips.

55
This Is Alateen

GOALS: ▶

Increase awareness of the Alateen program
- Introduce the Twelve Steps
- Encourage participation in Alateen

DESCRIPTION: ▶

Several members from an Alateen group visit the support group and discuss the Alateen program and how it helps them.

DIRECTIONS: ▶

Contact an Alateen group in your community to request speakers. These speakers can present the Alateen program and the Twelve Steps and share how these help them cope with the chemical dependence in their families. Be sure to save some time for questions at the end. If you think that your group members might be hesitant to ask questions, you might ask your group to make a list of questions ahead of time that you can give to the speakers.

NOTES: ▶

If possible, use Alateen speakers who aren't students in your school so that your guest speakers won't feel uncomfortable sharing. There isn't anything wrong with a speaker who is somewhat older than your support group members, either—the message still will come across and the speaker can become a role model for your group members.

If there isn't an Alateen meeting in your community, talk with members of Alanon about getting a meeting started. You can make these contacts through the A.A. hotline or clubhouse listed in the phone directory.

MATERIALS: ▶

None required, though you might want to have some Alateen materials on hand that group members could borrow.

56
Human Hotline

Stage: 3
Challenge: HIGH
Grades: ALL

GOALS: ▶
- Familiarize students with community resources
- Encourage students to reach out when they need help
- Provide emergency resources

DESCRIPTION: ▶
Group members construct a list of people and agencies that they can turn to when they need help. After role-playing a typical interaction, group members are asked to choose one person on their list and make an initial contact.

DIRECTIONS: ▶
Ask the group to make a list on the blackboard of people they could turn to when they are feeling lonely, frightened, or are in danger. This list should include friends, relatives, school staff, counselors, the police, crisis centers, and phone hot lines.

Once they've made this list, pass out blank note cards. On one side, group members should record community agencies and phone numbers; on the other side they should write down the names and phone numbers of close friends, relatives, school staff members, and counselors.

Ask group members to pick a person from their list whom they would feel comfortable asking for help. Pick someone in the group to role-play reaching out to one of the adults or organizations listed on her card. For example, Janna might have identified her history teacher as someone she trusts and respects. Someone else in the group role-plays the history teacher and Janna approaches her and says: "You know, Mrs. Johnson, sometimes things get pretty crazy around my house and I was wondering if I could talk to you when I'm feeling really upset. Like after school for a little while or something. Would that be okay?"

After everyone has had a chance to role-play asking for help, ask them to approach the person they chose sometime within the following week and talk with him or her in a fashion similar to what they practiced in their role-plays. The following week, the group can discuss these experiences.

NOTES:
If group members identify teachers as support people, you may wish to alert the faculty that they might be approached sometime in the following week.

MATERIALS:
Small note cards and telephone books.

57
What Do I Tell My Friends?

Stage: 2-3
Challenge: MODERATE
Grades: ALL

GOALS: ▶
- Reduce shame and embarrassment
- Minimize isolating behaviors

DESCRIPTION: ▶

Group members discuss a variety of approaches for dealing with the problem of friends becoming aware of a parent's chemical dependence.

DIRECTIONS: ▶

After introducing this topic, ask group members to give examples of when their parents' drinking or using behavior embarrassed them. Typical examples include a sleep-over occurring when Dad was drunk and started yelling, a time when a parent came to the school play and had fallen asleep from taking too many pills, or an occasion when a friend wanted to come over after school but this student wouldn't let him because he was afraid that his mother might be drunk. Write the students' examples on the blackboard as they are offered.

After there are at least ten examples, go back over the list and ask the group to identify at least one positive solution for each problem listed. For example, the group might decide that the best thing to do is just be honest—"It's his problem, not yours"—or that you should avoid asking the chemically dependent parent for rides home.

NOTES: ▶

Be prepared to offer both typical problems to list on the board as well as possible solutions to these problems if the group gets stuck. As much as possible, though, keep the responsibility on the group's shoulders to think of solutions to the problems they identify.

MATERIALS: ▶

None required.

58
Staying Safe

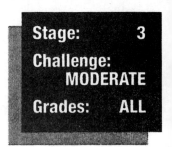

Stage: 3
Challenge: MODERATE
Grades: ALL

GOALS: ▶
- Help students create emergency plans
- Teach students the importance of protecting themselves

DESCRIPTION: ▶
Group members discuss different strategies for staying safe in dangerous situations in regards to the chemically dependent parent, and then construct a personal emergency plan.

DIRECTIONS: ▶
Ask group members to list a variety of dangerous situations in which children with chemically dependent parents are placed, such as physical abuse or riding in a car with a parent who has been drinking or using. Then give them the **My Emergency Plan** worksheet to complete (see following page). After they have completed the worksheet, ask students to share their answers with the rest of the group. Typical emergency plans can include going to a friend's house when the fighting starts, refusing to ride with the parent when he or she has been drinking, calling a relative when there is something wrong.

NOTES: ▶
Some group members will have more of a need for an emergency plan because some chemically dependent families are more turbulent than others. Where younger students are involved, concerns of the student must be weighed against rights of the parent. Telling twelve-year-old students to get out of the house when their parents are fighting might only generate more trouble for the students. Since each situation is different and there are few simple solutions, ask group members to consider the ramifications of their emergency plans: Will this really help them or just make things worse in the long run?

MATERIALS: ▶
My Emergency Plan worksheet.

My Emergency Plan

Living in a home where there's chemical dependence can sometimes make things dangerous for you. List three dangerous situations that have happened or could happen in the future:

Situation #1

Situation #2

Situation #3

Now for each of these three dangerous situations, think of two different plans—things you can do to take care of yourself and make sure you stay safe.

In situation #1, I can:

Or I can:

In situation #2, I can:

Or I can:

In situation #3, I can:

Or I can:

59
Learning How to Say "No"

GOALS: ▶
- Identify ways to resist peer pressure to use mind-altering chemicals
- Practice using these new skills

DESCRIPTION: ▶
Students identify, through group discussion and with help from the group leader, techniques for resisting peer pressure to use alcohol or other drugs. These new skills are practiced through role-playing.

DIRECTIONS: ▶
After introducing the topic, ask students to list different methods for resisting peer pressure to use alcohol or other drugs. Ask a group member to record these examples on the chalkboard. The examples can be both strategies the students have used before, or ones they think would work. Typical examples include saying "No thanks. I don't feel like it," walking away from the person offering the beer or joint, or saying "Naw. I've got to go home in an hour." If the group is having difficulties providing examples, you might want to ask them to think of a particular situation first and then think of the response. Ask them how they would handle someone offering them a joint out in the school parking lot, or at a party, for example.

Once they've listed a number of methods on the board, the group should choose one to role play. Ask for volunteers for different parts: one student to say "no", a student to offer the beer or joint, several others to play supporting roles such as other people at the party, and friends of either of the first two students.

Once the roles are assigned, give the group members a few minutes to create a short role-play. You might want to tell them to go over into the corner of the room, away from the rest of the group, to work out the details. When they are ready, they should act out the scenario for the rest of the group.

When they've finished the role-play, discuss the scenario with the group. Has anyone been in this type of situation before? Was it difficult or easy to handle? What are some other responses that could be used in this situation?

Act out new situations from the blackboard list with different group members.

NOTES: ▶
If your support group members are having a tough time getting into the character of their roles, you could help out by getting out there and playing a role, too. It can also be helpful to select group members who are natural clowns for the initial role-play. You might also want to provide props to make the scene realistic: an empty beer can, taped rock-and-roll party music, a steering wheel.

MATERIALS: ▶
Theatrical props, if desired.

60
Making Choices

GOALS: ▶
- Learn decision-making technique
- Practice decision-making process

DESCRIPTION: ▶ Students learn about, and then practice, healthy decision-making skills using real-life problems.

DIRECTIONS: ▶ Introduce this activity by encouraging group members to describe problems they've had in the past in which they had to decide on a course of action. Examples might include deciding whether to drink alcohol at a party, how to handle an overbearing friend, or what to do about the drinking problem of a family member.

Before handing out the **Making Choices** worksheet (see following page), explain the different steps to the decision-making process, using a situation that you or the group selects and the worksheet as a guide. Once the group understands the different steps, ask them to complete step one of the worksheet.

After everyone has identified a problem that they don't know how to handle, go around the group circle, asking everyone to share the problem they chose in step one. When a group member shares her problem, each member of group should volunteer a possible solution. She can record these solutions in step two. Steps three and four of the worksheet can then be completed individually. When everyone has finished step four, ask the group to share their worksheets. Challenge them to follow through on their chosen course of action sometime before the next group session so that, during the following session, the outcomes can be discussed and the final step of the worksheet can be completed.

MATERIALS: ▶ **Making Choices** worksheet

Making Choices

Step One: What is the problem?

Step Two: What are your possible choices? (Ask the group.)

    1.
    2.
    3.
    4
    5.
    6

Step Three: Think about your choices.

                positive aspects   negative aspects
    1.
    2.
    3.
    4.
    5.

Step Four: Decide which choice is the best for you.

Step Five: Follow through with this choice.

Step Six: Afterwards, reflect on the choice you made.
Looking back, was this really the best choice?

Will you do anything differently next time you're in this situation?

61
Does the Problem Affect Me?

GOALS: ▶
- Reduce denial of group members
- Encourage honest appraisal of the problem
- Increase group unity

DESCRIPTION: ▶ Group members complete a short questionnaire that focuses on how children are affected by a parent's chemical dependence. The remainder of the session is spent discussing the group members' answers.

DIRECTIONS: ▶ Pass out the **Questionnaires** (see following page) and ask students to answer each question honestly. After everyone has finished, ask students to share their answers with the rest of the group.

NOTES: ▶ Being mindful of the time remaining, ask group members for examples rather than simply "yes" or "no" answers. For example, with question number one you could ask, "Why are you concerned?" or "What bothers you about this person's drinking?"

This activity will be more successful if you call first on students who are already able to make an honest appraisal of the chemical dependence problem in their families. This will encourage other group members to share honestly.

MATERIALS: ▶ Questionnaire.

Questionnaire

PLEASE CHECK YES OR NO TO THE FOLLOWING QUESTIONS

	YES	NO
1. Are you concerned about a parent's, relative's or close friend's chemical use?	—	—
2. Do you spend a lot of time thinking about this person's chemical use?	—	—
3. Have you ever thought that this person has a problem with his or her chemical use?	—	—
4. Do you stay out of the house as much as possible because of this person's chemical use?	—	—
5. Are you afraid to upset this person because it may cause him or her to use more chemicals?	—	—
6. Do you feel that no one at home really loves you or cares what happens to you?	—	—
7. Are you afraid or embarrassed to bring your friends home because of a family member's chemical use?	—	—
8. Do you tell lies to cover up for this person's chemical use?	—	—
9. Have you ever wanted to talk to somebody about this person's chemical use?	—	—
10. Is your school work suffering because of this person's chemical use?	—	—

62
Taking Care of Me

GOALS:
- Identify different ways to take care of yourself
- Encourage group members to take care of themselves

DESCRIPTION: ▶
Group members make up a list of all the different things they can do that help them take care of themselves and then choose three that they can start to practice in their own lives.

DIRECTIONS: ▶

After discussing the importance of taking care of yourself, ask the group to make up a list of all the different things they can do that will help them to take care of themselves. This should be a long list. You can suggest any important ideas they forget. Here are some examples students usually mention:
- Get out of the house when the drinking starts.
- Go to Alateen or a church group.
- Talk with close friends about how I am feeling.
- Practice detaching.
- Find friends that help me feel good about myself.
- Talk with the school guidance counselor.
- Do something fun to get my mind off the problem at home.

When a student makes a suggestion, ask her for a specific example that helps make this suggestion more concrete for the rest of the group. It's also helpful to ask the student why her suggestion is a good idea—"Why should you talk about your feelings with close friends?" for example.

After the group has made an exhaustive list on the blackboard, ask everybody in the group to choose at least two suggestions from the list that both apply to their lives and that would be helpful for them to practice. Ask group members to explain why they chose those particular selections and if practicing these new behaviors will be easy or difficult.

NOTES: ▶
Anything that helps group members take their minds off the problem at home, helps them to feel good, and isn't damaging to themselves or others qualifies as taking care of themselves. This can include reading a joke book to talking with a counselor, from going for a long run to praying.

MATERIALS:
None required.

63
How the Problem in My Family Affects Me

GOALS:

- Increase awareness of effects of parental chemical dependence on students' feelings and behaviors
- Increase group unity

DESCRIPTION: ▶

Students identify and then discuss how they are personally affected by their parents' chemical dependence.

DIRECTIONS: ▶

First discuss various ways children can be affected by their parents' chemical dependence by asking group members for examples. List these examples on the blackboard.

Now ask group members to think about how they personally are affected by their parents' chemical dependence by making a list on a piece of paper. When they have finished writing, spend the remaining time sharing lists with the rest of the group.

NOTES: ▶

Resist the temptation to focus on making changes; the goal for this session is to encourage awareness of the problem. Personal changes springing from these awarenesses will come later. Don't rush it.

This activity is best saved until there is both intimacy in the support group and some understanding of chemical dependence.

MATERIALS:

Paper.

64 Detaching from the Problem

Stage: 3
Challenge: MODERATE
Grades: 9-12

GOALS: ▶
- Understand detaching
- Practice specific detaching skills

DESCRIPTION: ▶

Group members identify personal situations that they need to detach from and learn new skills they can use to detach from the problems at home.

DIRECTIONS: ▶

First, introduce the concept of detaching (see following page) and ask the students to identify previous experiences when their feelings and behaviors were affected by their parents' chemical dependence. Typical examples can include "When my Dad asks me to promise not to tell Mom he's been drinking, so I avoid her," or "At night when I'm watching TV and my Mom starts drinking and falls asleep next to me on the couch, I get angry." Note each example on the blackboard.

After everyone has shared situations pertaining to the chemical dependence in their family that they need to detach from, begin with the first situation on the blackboard and ask the group to think of different ways that they could detach themselves from the chemically dependent person's behavior.

When several different detaching strategies have been discussed by the group, ask the group member who identified the particular issue if any of these detaching methods seem workable. If she doesn't like any of the strategies that were discussed, ask her what strategy she would like to use. The goal is to help a group member choose a detaching strategy that seems workable to her. Typical scenarios will include a student deciding that from now on he won't argue with his Dad when his Dad is under the influence, or the student who realizes that giving her Mom a kiss after school everyday to see if she could smell alcohol on her Mom's breath only made her sad and angry when she discovered her mother had been drinking.

After the student who offered this situation has listened to possible solutions and has chosen one to use in the future, proceed with the next situation.

NOTES: ▶

If the group isn't able to form a detaching plan for a specific situation, you can offer them suggestions. As much as possible, though, allow the group to problem-solve group members' detaching needs. An excellent book that provides additional examples you can use in your support group is *Different Like Me* (see Resources section). It is important to stress the point that detaching is not turning your back on someone or loving this person less. Sometimes group members will be confused about this.

MATERIALS: ▶

None required.

For Your Information . . .

Detaching

When the chemically dependent people in group members' families are being particularly troublesome, they need to know how to back off and separate themselves from the problem. The secret lies in the recognition that they can't change their parents, but they can change how they react to the problem. This is called detaching, and it's an important skill for these students to learn. They need to understand that just because Dad is in a rotten mood or Mom is drinking again doesn't necessarily mean that they must also be upset. Their parent's problems don't have to be their problems, too.

An excellent description of detachment is found in the booklet called *Detachment, The Art of Letting Go While Living With an Alcoholic* by Evelyn Leite:*

> The feelings of anger, shame, and guilt associated with family alcoholism come from the constant confusion, conflict, unpredictability, inconsistency, mistrust, and sense of failure that each member experiences. The family victims seldom learn without outside help that they didn't cause the disease and they can't control it.

> Literally, to save and enjoy their lives, they need to do something positive, something that will help them focus on their own problems and the treatment they need to get well. They need to shift the focus of their attention from the alcohol and the alcoholic to themselves: to their problems, their reactive behavior, and what they can do for themselves in their own recovery from the family disease of alcoholism. To free themselves for these positive steps in their return to a healthy life, these family victims need to separate themselves from their reactive behavior and its causes. How? By developing the skill of *detachment*.

---

* For more information on this subject, you may also want to read the booklet *Detachment vs. Intervention: Is There a Conflict?* (see Resources section).

65
Is There a Problem Here?

GOALS: ▶

- Help group members assess the nature of the drinking problem in their families
- Identify how this problem affects group members

DESCRIPTION: ▶

The group discusses common characteristics of chemical dependence and its affects on the family.

DIRECTIONS: ▶

Ask group members to make a list of common characteristics of chemical dependence on the blackboard. Examples can include heavy drinking, hangovers, hidden bottles, frequent arguing, lost jobs, blackouts. If the group fails to mention significant items, bring them to their attention.

Once a thorough list has been made, go around the circle asking each group member to personalize this list by describing the various symptoms that she sees evidenced in her house.

NOTES: ▶

You should also point out that neither you, the group nor the student whose parent is being discussed can know for sure whether the parent is chemically dependent or not. The point is that the drinking or other drug usage is causing problems for each member of the group, and that is what's important. Remind the group, "If it's a problem for you, then it's a problem."

MATERIALS: ▶

None required.

66
My Own Chemical Use

GOALS:
- Complete self-assessments of students' chemical use
- Become aware of the risks of chemical use
- Familiarize group leaders with students' chemical use

DESCRIPTION:
Group members complete a worksheet that details their experiences with mind-altering chemicals. This information is then discussed in group.

DIRECTIONS:
Inform the group that because they're high risk for developing a problem with alcohol or other drugs, this session of group will focus on their own chemical use. Hand out the **Chemical History** worksheet (see following page), asking the students to complete it honestly and reminding them that the information on their sheets will remain confidential. When they are finished, spend the rest of the session discussing their answers. After a group member has shared his worksheet, offer your impressions concerning what he reported. If a student doesn't use alcohol or other drugs, be sure to support that position. If a student shares an extensive history of alcohol or other drug use, ask her how that affects her at school or home. Ask her if she wonders whether or not she will end up with a problem like her chemically dependent parent. Encourage input from the rest of the group by asking them what they think about her chemical use.

NOTES:
Group members will be much more honest if they are reassured that the information written on the worksheet won't be shared outside of group and that they can take the worksheets with them when group is finished.

   If, through this activity, you become concerned about a group member's chemical use, you may wish to meet with this student after group, share your concerns more directly, and make a referral to your school's student assistance program or school counselor *without sharing the specific contents of the student's worksheet.* This student should most likely be in a support group that focuses specifically on a student's own chemical use.* Students in trouble with their own chemical use won't be able to gain much from a support group that focuses on someone else's.

MATERIALS:
Chemical History worksheet.

* This type of support group, typically called a Drug Information Group, isn't addressed in this curriculum guide. It is discussed at length, however, in *Conducting Support Groups for Students Affected by Chemical Dependence* and in a curriculum guide similar to this one called *101 Support Group Activities for Teenagers at Risk for Chemical Dependence or Other Problems* (see Resources section).

Chemical History

This worksheet is a summary of your experiences with mind-altering chemicals—how much and how often, both past and present. Under the Past category, fill in how old you were when you first used that chemical, and then how much and how often you used during the first year. Under the Present category, fill in how much and how often you currently use that chemical. Do this for every chemical you have used on the list.

Name_____   Date_____

CHEMICAL	PAST			PRESENT		
(The first line is filled in as example.)	Age	Amount	Frequency	Amount	Frequency	
Alcohol	13	3 beers	once a week	6 beers	twice a week	
Alcohol (beer, wine, liquor)						
Marijuana (pot, hash, hash oil)						
Uppers (speed, crystal, crosstops)						
Downers (ludes, barbs, tranquilizers)						
Hallucinogens (LSD, acid, mushrooms)						
Inhalants (glue, gasoline, rush)						
Codeine (in cough syrup or in pain medication)						
Heroin (smack)						
Cocaine (snow, crack)						
PCP (angel dust)						
Other (specify)						

67
Do's and Don'ts

GOALS:
- Reinforce important lessons learned in group
- Provide a list of suggestions to which students can refer

DESCRIPTION:

Group members make a list of important lessons they have learned during group. This list is then photocopied so that everyone can take a copy home with them.

DIRECTIONS:

Ask the group to make a list on the blackboard of do's and don'ts they would suggest to other students who have a chemically dependent family member. Be sure to ask students to explain and cite examples of their suggestions as they offer them (see following page for a list of examples).

After recording these suggestions, type them on a notecard-size piece of paper and then make enough copies for all group members. The following week of group give them to group members and tell them they can keep these cards in their purses or wallets to refer to when they're having a difficult time dealing with the chemical dependence in their families.

NOTES:

It is more effective to make these cards seem more official by photocopying the suggestions onto heavyweight paper stock and laminating them in plastic. Since you will most likely have too many suggestions to fit on a small card, you might consider optically reducing the list with the photocopying machine.

You might also find that it's more effective to make the list solely from group's suggestions rather than from the examples included here. Furthermore, though it might seem like a good idea to pass out additional copies of this card in future support groups, it will be more effective for each group to construct their own list, rather than reading someone else's. Then the group has a sense of ownership of the ideas rather than following someone else's suggestions.

MATERIALS:

Notecards, plastic laminate.

Do's and Don'ts

1. Do talk about your feelings.

2. Do try to improve your life . . . even if the person with the drinking problem doesn't seem to want to change.

3. Do learn about how the problem affects you.

4. Do work on feeling better about yourself.

5. Do reach out to others for support.

1. Don't feel like the drinking problem is your fault.

2. Don't feel responsible for other people's problems.

3. Don't take out your frustrations on others.

4. Don't follow down the same path as the person with the drinking problem.

5. Don't let the drinking problem become your problem too.

68
Dear Andy

GOALS:

- Find solutions for problems common to living in a chemically dependent family
- Learn new coping skills

DESCRIPTION:

Group members read fictitious letters to an advice column and discuss solutions to the problems raised in these letters.

DIRECTIONS:

Taking turns, students should choose and then read aloud a letter from the samples provided (see following page). After reading a letter, the group discusses what advice it would give.

MATERIALS:

Sample letters.

Dear Andy Letters

Dear Andy:

My dad has a drinking problem. He doesn't live with us anymore. Since he's left, my mom is always too busy or tired to pay any attention to me. Instead she's always worrying about the bills and is sad or crabby most of the time. I feel like my dad forgot all about me and that I'm just one more problem for my mom. Now things have gotten bad at school 'cause I just don't care about homework or grades any more. My mom and me fight all the time and I feel angry, lonely, and confused.

                  John

Dear Andy:

My mom is an alcoholic. My parents have been divorced for three years and since my mom can't take care of me, I'm living with my dad. Dad is really angry with my mom. He says hurtful and angry things about her. I feel like I should defend her, but every time I do, Dad and me just end up fighting. What should I do to protect my mom?

                  Melanie

Dear Andy:

Almost twice a week, I listen to my parents fight. It's usually after Dad gets drunk. (He drinks almost every night.) I try to listen to figure out who's right and who's wrong. The problem is I don't get much sleep at night and I fall asleep in class the next day. I don't know what I should do about it.

                  Matthew

Dear Andy:

I've been over to a friend's house now several times to spend the night. He's starting to ask why I don't ask him over to spend the night or at least have supper. The reason I don't is I'm afraid that my mom will be drinking and do something to embarrass me in front of my friend. Should I ask my mom to promise not to drink?

                  Larry

Dear Andy:

Yesterday I forgot to put my bike in the garage and when my dad came home he just about ran it over. He started swearing at me and hitting me in the chest and the side of my head. He was drunk like he usually is. When Mom came out he stopped. This isn't the first time he's hit me. I feel like running away but I don't know where I'd go. What else could I do?

    Leigh

Dear Andy:

My older brother has a bad drug problem. Whenever our parents are gone, he's off in his room getting high or inviting friends over to party. A few days ago, they stole some liquor from my dad. He saw that it was gone and started accusing all of us kids. Now he's demanding someone confess. My brother told me that if I say anything, he'll never speak to me again. I don't want to narc on my brother, but I don't want to be blamed either.

    Sandra

Section E: Family Relationship Activities

Chemical dependence is often called the family disease. Because it affects everyone in the family. Honest communication is blocked, the children's emotional and sometimes physical needs aren't met consistently, while the dynamics of denial force everyone to pretend there's nothing wrong. Not surprisingly, family members react to this painful chaos, developing definite roles in their families over the years.

Some children with chemically dependent parents simply turn off their feelings (at least on the outside). They don't show much reaction to anything around them. Another role is characterized by anger. These kids appear angry most of the time: instead of feeling sad, they scowl; instead of feeling scared, they yell. Still other kids will become compulsive clowns. Everything is funny. They tease other students, they laugh at inappropriate times, they can't sit still. Another common role fools quite a few adults: the "everything's perfect" ploy—perfect grades, busy all the time, never a sad face.

It's important for support group members to realize that they are affected by their parent's chemical dependence, too. The activities in this section will help students understand just what these effects are.

69
Family Faces

GOALS: ▶
- Increase awareness of family dynamics
- Assess specific relationships within students' families

DESCRIPTION: ▶
Students complete a worksheet by drawing expressive faces for, and describing the relationship with, each member of their families.

DIRECTIONS: ▶
Hand out the **Family Faces** worksheet (see following page) and ask them to draw expressive features for each blank face. When they are finished with the faces, they should follow the instructions for the blank lines next to each face. When everyone has finished the worksheet, ask them to share their answers with the rest of the group.

QUESTIONS: ▶
- Do the moods of your family members change often? Why is this?
- Can you read the differing moods of your family?
- Which family members do you feel close to? Which ones are difficult for you to spend time with?

NOTES: ▶
When students are living with a stepparent, they might ask, for example, if they should designate their biological father or their stepfather (or Mom's live-in boyfriend) as "Dad." Instruct them to make their own choices, but to place the person they didn't select as "Dad" in the "other family" section of the worksheet.

MATERIALS: ▶
Family Faces worksheet.

Family Faces

FAMILY FACES

	words that describe this person	words that describe your feelings about this person
MOM ⭕		
DAD ⭕		

BROTHERS & SISTERS

⭕

⭕

⭕

OTHER FAMILY

⭕

⭕

70
Family Trees

GOALS: ▶
- Create a historical perspective of chemical dependence in the family
- Increase awareness of the degree of risk of group members becoming chemically dependent themselves

DESCRIPTION: ▶ Students create a family tree that identifies the relatives who have been affected by chemical dependence.

DIRECTIONS: ▶ Hand out large sheets of newsprint to group members and tell them they'll be drawing a form of a family tree. After writing their own name in the middle of the sheet, they should draw one connecting line up and one down and write their parents' names—one on top, the other on the bottom. After drawing circles around their parents' names, they should continue to make more connecting branches for their grandparents. After there are names and circles for these two generations, add aunts and uncles, great aunts and uncles, and even cousins if they wish. After all of these names have been added, students may also wish to add names of stepparents, in-laws, or live-in boyfriends or girlfriends of their parents.

Once their family tree has been constructed, ask group members to go back and identify any relatives with a drinking or drug problem by writing the word 'problem' inside the circle underneath this person's name. Time permitting, ask group members also to write a word or two in each circle of relatives without a drinking problem that describes this person's personality, such as moody, happy-go-lucky, or quiet (see following page for a sample Family Tree). Use the remaining time to discuss these family trees.

QUESTIONS: ▶
- How has chemical dependence impacted your extended family?
- Have you ever discussed your chemically dependent relatives with your parents?
- How has chemical dependence affected your family members who don't have a drinking problem?
- What are you doing to make sure you won't become chemically dependent?

NOTES: ▶ Since so many group members come from blended, and consequently complicated, families, concentrate first on the biological family. Students can add other family members as time allows.

MATERIALS: ▶ Large sheets of newsprint and markers.

Family Tree

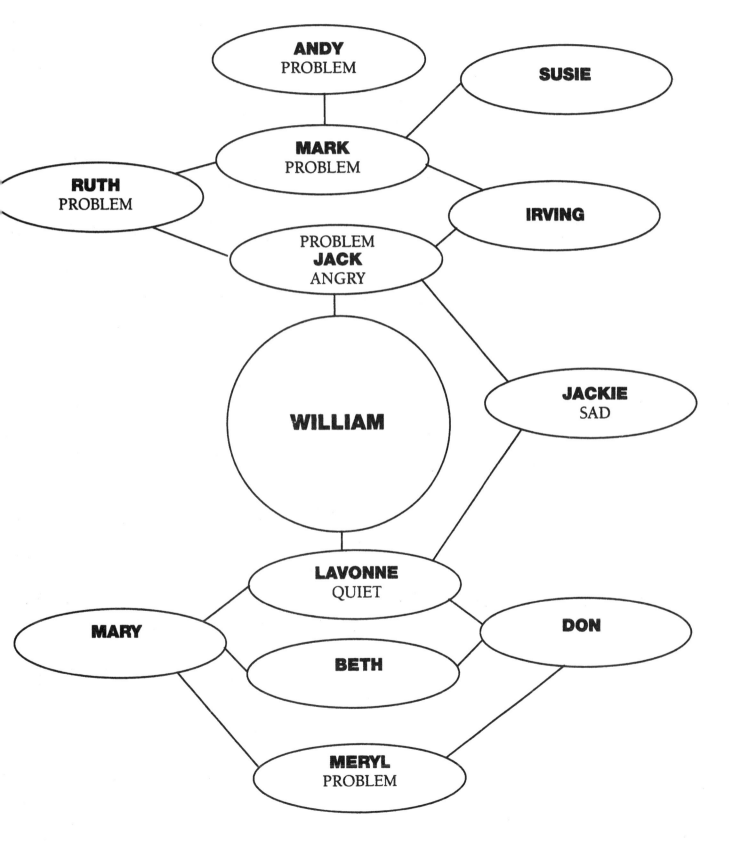

71
Family Collage

Stage: 2-3
Challenge: MODERATE
Grades: ALL

GOALS:
- Describe students' families
- Explore feelings related to family issues

DESCRIPTION:
Students make a collage depicting their families and family issues using pictures cut from magazines.

DIRECTIONS:
Place a large stack of various magazines in the center of the group circle. After giving everyone scissors, glue, and a sheet of construction paper, ask group members to page through the magazines and cut out pictures or words that describe their families, the problems that their families experience, and the students' reaction to their families. They can either paste on pictures and words as they find them or first cut out all of the pictures they will use and then begin to assemble the collage. Once the collages are finished, the remaining time can be spent discussing them.

QUESTIONS:
- What kind of feelings are represented in your collage?
- What are the problems in your family?
- What would you change in your family?
- Where are you in your collage?

NOTES:
You may wish to make this activity span two sessions—the first for making the collage and the second for group discussion.

MATERIALS:
Wide variety of magazines representing cultural diversity, sheets of construction paper, scissors, and bottles of white glue.

72
Family Sculpture

Stage: 3

Challenge: HIGH

Grades: 9-12

GOALS: ▶
- Help students understand their family dynamics
- Communicate nature of problems at home

DESCRIPTION: ▶
Students, using other group members, make a living sculpture of their own family.

DIRECTIONS: ▶
Tell group members that rather than trying to verbalize what is happening in their families, you would like them to show the rest of the group by making a human sculpture. Ask for a volunteer to begin by choosing group members to represent his family. He should also choose a group member to play himself as it's important that the student isn't an actor in his own family sculpture. One by one he should show these group members where to stand or sit, how to hold their bodies and what sort of facial expressions to wear. For example, he might put his alcoholic mother in the center holding her head down in shame, his angry father towering above and pointing his finger, his sister sitting looking off into the distance, and himself (played by another group member) running in circles around the family. Ask him to try to create positions for all members of the group (perhaps as uncles or family friends) so that one or two students aren't left on the outside.

When everyone is in place, ask them to hold their positions in the sculpture for a minute or two so the entire group can form some impressions. Then the actors can relax a bit and the group can talk about the sculpture using the questions below as a guide. Depending on the time remaining, continue this activity by creating additional family sculptures.

QUESTIONS: ▶
- How did your role feel to you?
- What were the feelings displayed in this family?
- What did group members outside the family observe?
- What is happening in this family?
- Who is protecting whom?
- What needs to happen for this family to get better?
- What can (the student whose family was reenacted) do to take care of himself?

CONTINUED ON NEXT PAGE

NOTES:

This can be a very intense activity, not appropriate for a beginning group. It's especially important, with an activity such as this, that you maintain a clear distinction between support and therapy. This activity is designed to create insight into family dynamics and to help group members identify new ways of relating to their families. It's not to be used as a catharsis for exposing unresolved issues or venting powerful emotions, as could be accomplished in a therapeutic group.

MATERIALS:

None required.

73
Family Rules

GOALS: ▶
- Increase awareness of unspoken family rules
- Discover similarities in families

DESCRIPTION: ▶

Group members discuss their family rules.

DIRECTIONS: ▶

Begin a discussion of the variety of rules that are present in families by asking the students for examples. Typically, they will mention rules such as curfew, keeping their room clean, no smoking. Then point out there are many other rules that, though never discussed, are present, such as the importance of always being in a good mood, not bothering Mom when she's been drinking, or not talking about Uncle Richard's drug problem. Ask students for examples of these types of rules that exist in their houses. After they have mentioned a few examples, ask them to make a list of the rules, both stated and implied, that are a part of their families. When everyone has finished, ask them to share their lists with the rest of the group, giving an example of each rule as it is named.

NOTES: ▶

Though it will sometimes be the natural tendency of the group, try to steer the discussion away from complaining about the unfairness of curfew and other similar rules and instead concentrate on the covert, emotional rules of a family system.

MATERIALS: ▶

Paper.

74
Family Position

GOALS:

- Identify role in family system
- Evaluate strengths and weaknesses of this role
- Discuss methods for avoiding rigid roles

DESCRIPTION:

After explaining the roles children from a chemically dependent family often develop, group members identify their roles in their own families.

DIRECTIONS:

Begin this session by presenting information describing the different roles that children from a chemically dependent home often develop (see following page for information). Once group members understand these various roles, go around the circle asking group members to identify which role they identify with and, time permitting, which roles match different members of their families.

QUESTIONS: ▶

- What role do you play in your family?
- What advantages and disadvantages does this role have?
- What can you do to avoid getting stuck in this role?
- What roles do other members of your family play?

NOTES: ▶

If a student is unable to decide which role he sees himself in, ask the group to make suggestions. You might also want to offer your input here since you will most likely, after interacting with this student in group for awhile, have an impression of the role this student has adopted.

MATERIALS: ▶

None required.

For Your Information . . .

Family Positions

In most families, the children adopt loosely defined roles. Often the first born is the mature one, the child who is supposed to set an example for younger siblings; just as often, the youngest is forever seen as the baby of the family. In a dysfunctional family affected by parental chemical dependence, the children develop roles that become rigid and problematic. These roles are often hyperextensions of the more normal, natural roles and, once learned, are often carried into adult life. The tragedy here is that the now-grown child of an alcoholic still leads his or her life as defined by the role taken on during childhood. This is not unlike a Vietnam veteran, the war long over, still waking up with night sweats or flinching with each loud noise.

The following roles have been given titles originally coined by Sharon Wegscheider-Cruse, but behind these titles are four basic postures or reactions to the drinking problem: being very good, being rebellious, being apathetic, or being funny. Note that the roles are presented in a specific order. Often the roles can be tied to birth order, with the first born being the family hero, and so on. This isn't always the case, but it's true often enough that you should point this out to your group members.

THE FAMILY HERO
- Always does what's right; afraid of making any mistakes
- Super-achiever in school and sports
- Responsible for everything and everyone
- Often takes over parenting role

THE REBEL
- Hostile, tough, and defiant
- Often in trouble at school or home
- Usually at odds with the family hero
- Associates with the "partying" crowd

THE LOST CHILD
- Loner, daydreamer, quiet
- Spends most of the time reading books or watching TV
- Never attracts attention to self
- Very active fantasy life

THE MASCOT
- Immature, cute, hyperactive
- Does anything for a laugh or attention
- Class clown
- Short attention span and learning disabilities

75
What Would I Change at Home?

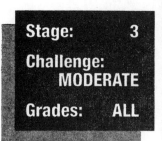

Stage: 3
Challenge: MODERATE
Grades: ALL

GOALS: ▶
- Recognize family strengths and weaknesses
- Determine what can be changed and what can't
- Make a plan for bringing about these changes

DESCRIPTION: ▶
Group members discuss both likes and dislikes concerning their home environment and family members. After deciding what is within their control to change, group members make action plans to bring about some of these changes.

DIRECTIONS: ▶
Encourage the group to list the things they can't stand about their family, both collectively and individually. Keep the focus related to the chemical dependence in the family. Ask them to write this list down on a piece of paper. Common answers include, "Whenever my Dad's drinking, he gets real mean." "I hate it that my Mom never stands up to my older brother when he comes home high and starts yelling at her." "I wish our family would be happier."

Once they have written down these dislikes, ask them to review the list and then place a check by the examples that are beyond their control to change. Most likely they will eliminate most of their lists—understandably so, since they can't force their mothers to quit drinking, or kick their fathers' girlfriends out of the house.

Now point out to the group that there are some things they can do about these situations. The key lies in the students' reaction. For example, instead of staying home and watching their mother get drunk, these students could call up a friend and get out of the house.

Now ask them, for each item on their list, to think of something they can change about how they react to the situation. If a group member is unable to come up with an alternative reaction, ask the rest of the group for ideas.

To finish this session, ask the group members to pick one situation from their lists that they are willing to work on throughout the next week by practicing their alternative reaction. During the following week of group, group members can discuss their progress with this assignment.

NOTES: ▶
If the group isn't already familiar with the serenity prayer, this session would be an excellent opportunity to introduce it:

> God, grant me the serenity to accept the things I cannot change
> the courage to change the things I can
> and the wisdom to know the difference.

MATERIALS: ▶
Paper.

76
Divorce Discussion

GOALS:

- Encourage honest discussion about divorce
- Identify problems and solutions related to divorce

DESCRIPTION:

The group room is split into two halves representing yes and no. The leader asks discussion questions and group members indicate their response by standing in either half of the group room.

DIRECTIONS:

Use masking tape to make a line on the group room floor. Tell students that one side is the "yes zone" and the other is the "no zone." Furthermore, the farther from the line they stand, the more strongly they are responding to the question. Begin the activity by reading one of the questions from the **Divorce Discussion** question list (see following page) and then asking group members to position themselves in the room according to their responses. After everyone is still, ask group members to explain their answer to the question. Encourage group discussion rather than short responses to the question.

MATERIALS:

Divorce Discussion questions.

Divorce Discussion Questions

- Is it hard on children when their parents get divorced?

- Should parents stay together for the sake of the children?

- Should parents decide who the children should live with?

- Is a drinking or drug problem a good reason to get divorced?

- Does a divorce solve the problems the parents were having?

- Should parents have to see a marriage counselor before they get divorced?

- Should a parent be denied the chance to see his or her children?

- Should custody rights usually be in favor of the mother?

- If your parents are divorced, was the divorce difficult for you?
  If your parents aren't divorced, would a divorce be difficult for you?

- If your parents are divorced, are you glad they are?
  If your parents aren't divorced, do you wish they were?

77
Dinner Table Theater

GOALS: ▶

- Increase understanding of family dynamics
- Help students identify various roles in their families

DESCRIPTION: ▶

Group members take turns role-playing their families at the dinner table, using support group members to act as their families.

DIRECTIONS: ▶

Explain to the students that it can be helpful to look at the interactions of their families from a distance rather than always being caught up in the emotional goings-on. And this activity affords a picture of students' families in a classic setting—the dinner table.

Ask for a volunteer to have her family role-played and, using the support group as family members, ask this volunteer to assign roles to each member of the group, including someone to play her own role. All significant members of this student's family should be included in the role-play. She will also need to instruct each group member how they should act in their role. This is best accomplished by describing the personality of this family member, and how he or she typically behaves at the dinner table. The volunteer should position her family members around an imaginary table and, once familiar with their roles, they should spend five minutes interacting (or not interacting, as the case may be) as a family. If there are extra group members without an assigned role, they can form a circle outside of the dinner table and observe the family carefully, being ready to offer observations afterwards.

When the role-play is finished, discuss the family that was role-played.

QUESTIONS: ▶

- What was happening in this family?
- What were the interaction patterns in this family?
- How did your role feel to you?
- What could (the volunteer whose family was being role-played) do in order to improve her home situation?

CONTINUED ON NEXT PAGE

NOTES:

This activity, if used inappropriately, could cross the line from support into therapy. The goal of this activity is for students to become more aware of how their family works and what their role in the family is. Since these role-plays can bring some painful feelings and issues to the fore, let the student whose family is being observed set the boundaries. Be sensitive and don't push. This activity is not for a beginning or immature group. Rather, it's for a group of students who are working together well as a group and are able to act out roles other than their own.

Since it will require approximately twenty minutes for each role-play (ten minutes assigning and explaining roles, five minutes acting, and five minutes discussion), most likely the group will be able to finish two role-plays at most during a session of group.

MATERIALS:

None required, although you'll find props such as a table and dishware make the role-playing easier for students.

78
A Letter to My Parent

Stage: 3
Challenge: HIGH
Grades: ALL

GOALS: ▶
- Clarify the problem and concerns a student has about a parent's chemical dependence
- Encourage expression of feelings

DESCRIPTION: ▶ Group members write a letter to their chemically dependent parent describing how they are affected and what they need. These letters aren't sent, but are destroyed in a ritualistic fashion.

DIRECTIONS: ▶ Ask group members to write a letter to their parent who has the drinking problem. After making sure they understand that these letters won't be sent to their parent, tell them to communicate all the things they would like to say but can't. This might include telling their father how much they hate his drinking, or their mother how worried they are, or talking about how they wish things could be at home. These letters will naturally be diverse and personal, but the key is for the students to express things they otherwise wouldn't be able to. When everyone is finished writing, ask students who are comfortable doing so to read their letters to the group.

There is a rather ceremonious and symbolic way to destroy these letters. After a student has read her letter—either out loud or to herself—ask her to fold the letter in half and then rip up the letter. But for each rip of the folded letter, she should tell the group something that she is doing or will start doing to take care of herself, such as talking about her feelings, avoiding arguing with her mother when her mother is drunk, or getting her homework done even though things are crazy at home.

MATERIALS: Paper.

79
Five Things I Appreciate about My Parents

Stage: 2-3

Challenge: LOW

Grades: ALL

GOALS: ▶
- Avoid stereotyping the chemically dependent parent
- Reinforce positive aspects of both parents

DESCRIPTION: ▶
Students are encouraged to identify and discuss positive aspects of their chemically dependent parents.

DIRECTIONS: ▶
Begin this activity by discussing with the group how the disease of chemical dependence can make a good person seem bad because the drinking behavior gets in the way of the real person. Then ask group members to list five positive qualities for both of their parents. Examples might include "When he's sober he's fun to be around," "Sometimes my mom will talk to me about what's going on with her and even ask me how I'm feeling," or "My dad always takes us on great summer vacations." After they have completed their lists, ask them to share their answers with the group.

QUESTIONS: ▶
- Have there been periods of time when your parents' behaviors were better or worse?
- Have you ever told your parents what you appreciate about them? Is that something that you could do in the future?

NOTES: ▶
If a group member has more than two parents—stepparent, live-in boyfriend— encourage them to write about whomever they wish.

MATERIALS: ▶
Paper.

80
Fantasy Day

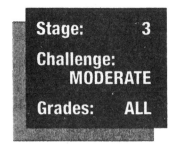

Stage: 3
Challenge: MODERATE
Grades: ALL

GOALS: ▶
- Help students realize positive qualities about their chemically dependent family member
- Encourage discussion of negative feelings

DESCRIPTION: ▶

Group members plan a fantasy day with their chemically dependent parent.

DIRECTIONS: ▶

Ask the group members to think for a moment about enjoyable activities they once did, but no longer do, with their chemically dependent parent. Maybe a group member used to go fishing regularly with his dad, or a group member and her mom would spend a couple of hours just laughing and talking. If a student can't remember anything enjoyable that he used to do, then have him choose something that he would like to do with this parent.

Pass around paper and ask them to plan out an entire day with this parent, or the entire family if they wish. They can do anything at all: go to an amusement park, fish, spend the afternoon playing cards.

When everyone has finished, ask them to share their fantasy day with the rest of the group.

QUESTIONS: ▶
- What is it that you miss in your relationship with your parent?
- Can you talk to him or her about what you miss?
- How did you feel during these past activities?

NOTES: ▶

Some group members might say that they don't want to spend any time with their chemically dependent parent. When this is the case, ask them to remember a time when their relationship was pleasant with this parent and to recall and then write about an activity during that time period.

It's especially important to be sensitive to issues of abuse during this activity. If there is a student in your group who was abused by her chemically dependent father, for example, it wouldn't be a good idea to ask this girl to plan a fantasy day with her father. Instead, let her plan a day with the family member of her choice.

MATERIALS: ▶

Paper.

Section F: Physical Motion Activities

Young people have lots of energy, and it's natural for them to express themselves with their bodies, with laughter, and with movement. The activities in this section focus on movement rather than thinking, nonverbal rather than verbal communication. You'll find them a great help in getting an otherwise hesitant group to begin interacting together.

Some of the activities challenge group members' trust levels, while other activities simply are about playing and laughing. Children from chemically dependent homes certainly need a lot more of this.

81
Dancing Introductions

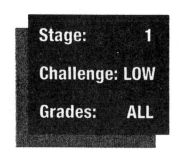

Stage: 1
Challenge: LOW
Grades: ALL

GOALS:
- Familiarize group members with each other
- Reduce nervousness and tension

DESCRIPTION:
Group members introduce themselves by giving their names in conjunction with a body movement.

DIRECTIONS:
Tell group members that they're going to play a game that will help them all remember each others' names. Ask them to count the syllables in their names and then create a series of body movements that follow the rhythm of their names. For example, Josephine has three syllables in it, so you need to create a three-movement dance: maybe swing an elbow (Jo), then snap your fingers (se), and then finish with a big hop (phine).

After giving them all time to create their own name dance, ask someone to start. Once he has given his name dance, allow him to choose the next student. This person must recite the previous name dances before she does her own. Since the last person has the most difficult task ahead of her, you might want to ask the first person in the name dance chain to make the body movements while a volunteer recites all the names.

NOTES:
Students may be uncomfortable beginning this activity. If so, you'll find it helpful to role-model the desired behavior and then choose a group member who is a natural 'ham' to go next.

MATERIALS:
None required.

82
Responsi-ball

GOALS: ▶
- Encourage personal disclosure
- Create group intimacy

DESCRIPTION: ▶
Group members play a ball game that requires self-disclosure when the ball is dropped.

DIRECTIONS: ▶
With everyone sitting in a circle, explain to the group that they're to pass the ball back and forth in the circle without it touching the ground. They should hit the ball as in a game of volleyball—not throw it as if they were playing catch. When the ball hits the floor, the last two people to touch the ball—the one who hit it and the one to whom it was hit—must decide who's responsible for the ball falling to the floor. This person must then share something about herself with the group, such as what she likes to do in her spare time, who her favorite musician is, how many siblings she has. If the two can't decide who was responsible, then the group should choose (or you could ask both players to share something about themselves). The game continues in this fashion for the remainder of the session.

NOTES: ▶
The ball for this game should be very light, such as a foam rubber ball or even crumpled-up tissue paper with a plastic bag cover. Balloons rarely hit the ground, so little sharing takes place.

MATERIALS: ▶
Lightweight ball.

83
The Growing Tree

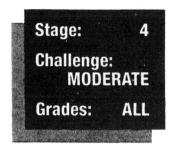

Stage: 4
Challenge:
   MODERATE
Grades: ALL

GOALS:

- Provide a challenge that must be solved through cooperative efforts
- Demonstrate emotional growth of the group

DESCRIPTION: ▶

Group members sculpt a tree using their bodies and, as the tree grows, they identify past growth experiences in their group.

DIRECTIONS: ▶

Briefly discuss the growth cycle of a tree with the group members, such as how a tree miraculously grows from a small fragile seed into a strong and beautiful living thing. Then challenge students to form a tree as a group, using their bodies for the trunk and branches. As much as possible, let the group solve the problems of how the trunk will be formed, who will be the branches, and which person will be the tip of the tree.

With the addition of each group member to the tree, this person must identify something that happened that signified growth either in the group as a whole or for this person individually. For example, as Marianne steps out to be the base of the tree, she might mention how she saw the group loosen up and become comfortable talking after the first week of group, though at first everyone was nervous and protective. Before James climbs up the bodies already in place to join the tree as a branch, he might tell how helpful it was for him to be able to talk about how concerned he is about his mother's drinking.

Continue this process until everyone has shared an observation about the growth of the group and is part of the group tree.

QUESTIONS: ▶

- How have you grown personally during this group?
- How has this group as a whole grown? How can you tell?
- How does this growth feel to you?

NOTES:

You may wish to photograph the completed group tree and make copies for everyone in group to keep as a remembrance of the growing and learning they did while in group.

MATERIALS:

None required.

84
Trust Falls

GOALS:

- Explore personal trust issues
- Increase level of trust in the group

DESCRIPTION: ▶

Group members are confronted with the issues of fear and trust by challenging themselves to fall back into the arms of other group members.

DIRECTIONS: ▶

This game can be played at a variety of levels, from simply standing stationary and falling backwards, to climbing up on a platform some three to four feet off the ground and falling back into the arms of the entire group.

At the first level, ask group members to pair off and take turn falling into each other's arms. When a student falls, he should have his arms at his sides, his eyes closed and his body straight and stiff like a board. His partner should stand several feet behind him—ready to catch him when he slowly falls backward. This is more frightening than it might seem! Once everyone has had a turn at falling, bring the group back into a circle and discuss this activity.

An advanced form of this activity requires the use of a gymnasium, some floor mats, and a platform three to four feet in height. Place the platform in front of several thick mats for padding (wrestling mats, gymnastic mats, or mattresses all work well). The first volunteer stands on top of the platform and the rest of the group stands in two rows below the platform, facing each other, and interlocks hands so that a trough (which needs to be as long as the students are tall) of catching arms is formed. A good way to lock hands is to have everyone grab their left wrists with their own right hands, and then to reach across to their partners facing them and grab their partner's right wrists with their own left hands. When done correctly, each facing pair of students has formed a small square with their hands.

The student should then fall back—eyes shut, body stiff, back first—into the arms of the entire group. After landing, the group can cradle the group member in a big hug before propping her up on her feet. Everyone is invited to take a turn falling, and afterwards the activity should be discussed.

QUESTIONS: ▶

- Was it uncomfortable to trust the group?
- How does it feel to put your care in the hands of others?
- Who are the people around you that you trust?
- Do you wish you were more trusting of other people?
- Is it a good idea to be more trusting of others? Why?

NOTES: ▶

The advanced version of this activity should only be attempted when there are enough people to catch the falling student safely. Six people catching is the absolute minimum—eight is much better. It's also important to have mats underneath, just in case someone were to fall through the group's arms. The ideal location for this activity is the corner of a gymnasium where the mats and a platform can be easily set up.

Make sure to stick up for any group members who don't want to fall—they shouldn't be intimidated into doing something that they don't want to do.

MATERIALS: ▶

For the advanced form, gym mats and a platform.

85
Toy Day

GOALS: ▶
- Encourage playfulness
- Help group members realize the importance of recreation

DESCRIPTION: ▶
Group members bring toys to group and, after a short discussion on the importance of play, the entire session is devoted to playing with toys.

DIRECTIONS: ▶
During the week before this session, ask all group members to bring at least one toy to the next group session. Group leaders should also bring a number of toys as some students will forget theirs (or doubt your sincerity). Discuss how simple, uncomplicated playing—for both young and old alike—is important. Point out that some children, when growing up in a chemically dependent family, don't get chances to just be kids and have fun. Instead, they become the surrogate parent, babysitting every day while their mother is down at the bar, or hiding in their bedrooms out of fear of verbal and physical abuse.

Once the students understand why the group is focusing on playing with toys, lay out your toys in a pile in the center of the group room. Go around the room, asking group members to show and explain the toys that they brought to group. Now begin to play. Encourage hesitant group members to follow suit or ask them to join in play with you. Reserve a few minutes at the end of this session to talk about how this activity felt.

NOTES: ▶
Be prepared for resistance. Once the activity is understood, you should just start playing. The group will follow suit as soon as they realize that you're serious.

MATERIALS: ▶
Toys. The more, the better.

86
Feelings Tag

GOALS: ▶
- Increase feelings vocabulary
- Increase awareness of variety of feelings

DESCRIPTION: ▶ Group members play a game of tag, shouting feeling words to avoid getting caught.

DIRECTIONS: ▶ This activity requires a large open area, preferably a small gymnasium, though you could be outside. If the area is too large, mark off some boundaries. Choose one student to be "it" first. This variation of tag is unique in that when the person who is "it" approaches someone else, that person can avoid being tagged by standing still and shouting a feeling word, such as angry, sad, or anxious. If the shouted feeling word is an uncommon one, the person who is "it" can challenge the group member to define the word or give an example. If the group member defines the word correctly (allow the rest of the group to monitor this), the person who is "it" then must move on and try to catch someone else. If the person incorrectly defines the word he or she shouted, then this person is now "it." Of course, if a person is tagged before they shout a feelings word, they are automatically "it."

As the game continues, the next person shouting out a feeling word must choose a new emotion. If a feeling word is shouted that has already been used, the person who is "it" can ignore the shout and tag him or her. This new person is now "it." When the group runs out of feeling words completely, start the game over.

NOTES: ▶ Group leaders should be out there playing, too!

MATERIALS: ▶ A large room where students can run around. You might also want to bring along a **Feelings Poster** (see Activity 17 or Appendix A for a list of feeling words) to help students.

87 Pulse

Stage: 1-3
Challenge: LOW
Grades: ALL

GOALS:
- Encourage group cooperation
- Provide noncompetitive recreation

DESCRIPTION:

One student stands in the center of the group circle while the remaining students join hands and pass a squeeze around the circle. The student in the center tries to locate this "pulse."

DIRECTIONS:

Ask group members to form a tight circle sitting cross-legged and holding hands. Tell the group that the object of this game is to pass a "pulse" around the circle without getting caught. This pulse is represented by the squeezing of hands. When a group member feels her right hand getting squeezed, for example, she then passes the pulse on by squeezing the group member's hand on her left. In this way the pulse is passed around the circle. The job of the person in the center is to catch the pulse after someone has received it, but before she has gotten rid of it.

Once the group has gotten the hang of passing the pulse, show them how they can reverse the direction of the pulse by squeezing back the same hand that squeezed theirs. This makes it much more difficult, but not impossible, for the person in the center to catch the pulse.

Once everyone is familiar with the game, start by asking someone to be in the center of the circle. Ask a student who is out of view of the person in the center to start the pulse. Once the pulse is moving, the student in the center is free to spin around and try to catch the pulse by pointing to someone and saying this person's name when he thinks she has the pulse. If he's correct, these two switch places and a new round starts; if he wasn't correct, the game continues.

MATERIALS:

None required.

158 / Section F: Physical Motion Activities

88
Grumpy

GOALS: ▶
- Provide noncompetitive recreation
- Break up the intensity of other group sessions

DESCRIPTION: ▶

Group members try to make one designated person laugh.

DIRECTIONS: ▶

Explain to the group that this game involves trying hard to keep a straight face despite the antics performed by the rest of the group. Ask for a volunteer to be "it" first. She should sit in the center of the circle while the rest of the group tries their best to make her laugh or crack a smile, but without touching her in any way. Group members should take turns trying to evoke a laugh, working around the circle. Whomever is successful in making her laugh gets to be in the center next.

After playing this game for most of the group session, spend some time talking about laughter and its benefits. Ask the group to think about and then discuss in what situations they can let go and laugh.

MATERIALS: ▶

None required.

89
Two Coyotes and a Rabbit

GOALS: ▶
- Provide noncompetitive recreation
- Encourage students to talk about themselves

DESCRIPTION: ▶

Group members play a chase game using three balls and talk about themselves when they are caught.

DIRECTIONS: ▶

Ask group members to stand and form a circle. Throw two basketballs out into the circle and ask group members to begin passing them around. These two basketballs are the coyotes and they can only be passed to neighboring group members—not across the circle. Once the group has gotten accustomed to these basketballs moving around the circle, throw out the volleyball. Tell the group that this ball, being the rabbit, can jump across the circle as well as move around the circle. Now all three balls will be moving in the circle. The object of the game is to avoid having the coyotes catch the rabbit, which occurs when a group member is holding the rabbit and is also passed one or both coyotes. If one coyote catches the rabbit, the game stops momentarily and the group member who was holding the rabbit must tell something about himself. If both coyotes catch the rabbit, the game pauses and the rest of the group creates a question for the group member who was holding the rabbit to answer.

NOTES: ▶

If this game is played in the group room, put any breakables, like lamps or vases, away for safe keeping. Playing this game in a gymnasium or other recreation area is preferable because sometimes the playing can get a little wild. Another idea would be to use softer and lighter balls, such as beach balls and a foam rubber ball.

MATERIALS: ▶

Two basketballs and one volleyball.

Section G:
Stress-reduction Activities

Young people living with chemical dependence in their family experience more than their share of stress. Verbal and physical fights, fears of the house being set on fire, financial instability, divorce, physical or sexual abuse, and moving to new cities are all-too-common experiences for these children. For most young people, home is a safe place to retreat from the harsh realities of the world, but for many young people with chemical dependence in their families, home isn't a refuge.

To make matters worse, these young people don't know how to cope with stress constructively because they don't have any role models at home. Mom drinks because of her stress; Dad yells and eats too much. Fortunately, in a support group we can teach these students how to recognize and cope with their personal stress.

90
Coping with Stress

Stage: 2-3
Challenge: MODERATE
Grades: ALL

GOALS:
- Evaluate personal stress level
- Learn variety of stress-reducing techniques

DESCRIPTION: ▶

Group members discuss a number of strategies for alleviating stress in their lives.

DIRECTIONS: ▶

Begin a discussion about stress—where it comes from and what happens to us when we're feeling it—by asking students to identify common stress-producing events, such as taking a test, going to a new school, or a parent returning home from a chemical dependence treatment center. Then ask them to describe what happens when stress builds up in their bodies. Examples can include sleeplessness, headaches, irritability.

Using the blackboard, ask the group to make a list of different things they do when they are feeling stressed. At this point, don't judge the effectiveness of their strategies. Typical examples include running, staring at the wall, fighting, talking about the stress, screaming into a pillow. When they are finished offering examples, ask the group to decide which of the strategies are counterproductive—that is, either don't reduce the stress or may even increase it. For example, screaming at others when you're tense produces guilt and additional stress; staring at the wall and brooding is a passive response that does little to alleviate the problem. Erase those examples the group agrees are counterproductive.

For the remaining list, ask the person who mentioned the example to explain how he uses it in his life—under what circumstances and what the outcome is. When all the remaining examples have been discussed, ask group members to choose one strategy to use the next time they are feeling stressed. Discuss which strategies they chose and in what situations they will use it.

NOTES:

If the group isn't able to produce very many different strategies for dealing with stress, be prepared to offer some for consideration. Here's a partial list: Running, talking with a friend, screaming into a pillow, writing in a journal, limiting responsibilities, spending all day in a park, snoozing in the sun, playing sports, meditating, practicing relaxation, yoga, deep breathing, daydreaming, reading a joke book, hanging out with friends.

MATERIALS:

None required.

91
Positive Imagery

Stage: 3
Challenge: LOW
Grades: ALL

GOALS: ▶
- Increase positive thinking patterns
- Reduce stressful feelings

DESCRIPTION: ▶
Group members are taught how to practice imagining positive thoughts about themselves and personal situations.

DIRECTIONS: ▶
Introduce the concept of critical and negative self-talk by listing some examples of how people are quick to put themselves down and judge themselves harshly. It would be especially helpful to give any personal examples of your own negative self-talk. Common examples include "I'll never get it right," "I'm not as attractive as she is," or "I'll probably mess up this speech I have to give in front of the class." Ask group members to share examples of their own negative thinking.

Tell the group that since these negative thoughts can affect both their feelings and behavior, you are going to teach them a method for thinking positive thoughts and imagining positive outcomes for situations in which they are involved.

First, ask group members to think of situations or common thought patterns in which they usually envision a negative outcome or are self-critical, such as worrying whether their friends like them, thinking that their parents are never going to quit drinking, or thinking that they're ugly. Then read the **Positive Imagery Script** on the following page.

After the positive imagery exercise, when everyone is back together in a circle, ask them to discuss their imaginary journeys.

Tell the group that they can use positive imagery whenever they are worrying about something or are giving themselves negative messages. All it takes is a minute or two to imagine a different, positive outcome.

QUESTIONS:
- What was the negative situation you imagined?
- What was the positive outcome for your situation?
- How did that outcome feel?
- Was it difficult to imagine a positive ending?

MATERIALS:
Positive Imagery Script.

Positive Imagery Script

First, they all need to find a spot, preferably on the floor, where they can be comfortable. Once everyone is settled, dim the lights and read the following script to them:

"I want you to close your eyes and move your body around a bit to make sure that you are settled and comfortable. Now breathe in deeply and slowly a few times. Each time you exhale, feel your body getting a little heavier and heavier. Imagine the tension in your body being exhaled right along with each breath. (Give them 20 seconds or so to relax.)

Now that you are relaxed, I want you to imagine the situation that you are worried about. Place yourself back in this situation. Imagine your surroundings, any other people who are present, the colors, the sounds. Now instead of things going wrong, imagine a great finish to this situation—the best possible outcome. You're happy, everything works out, there's nothing left to worry about. Stay with these good feelings for a minute. (Give them a minute or so to do this task.)

Now, I want you to come back to this group room. Listen to the sounds you hear in this room, go ahead and stretch a little if you want to. When you feel ready, open your eyes and join the group circle. **"**

92
Where's the Stress in My Body?

GOALS: ▶
- Identify stressors
- Create awareness of personal reaction to stress
- Learn how to deal with stress

DESCRIPTION: ▶ Students draw outlines of their bodies and then locate and write descriptions of how stress feels to them.

DIRECTIONS: ▶ Begin a discussion about stress, focusing on how our physical bodies can react to stress. Students may describe stress manifested in their bodies as headaches, knotted stomachs, or pain in their lower back, for example.

Pass out large sheets of newsprint and ask group members to trace each other's outlines. When finished, ask them to write the different stressors they experience on the outside of their body outline, and then to describe the different ways in which their bodies respond to stress with arrows, pictures, and words. For example, a student might identify tests, her father, dating, and starting a new class as stressors and, also on the paper, she might draw an arrow to her forehead and describe the headaches she gets whenever she is feeling uptight about her father's drinking and arrows to her fists and describe how she always clenches her fists when she is nervous.

After everyone has finished, use the remaining time to discuss the drawings, asking group members to think of positive ways that help them deal with their stress.

QUESTIONS: ▶
- How does stress feel to you?
- How can you tell when you are stressed?
- What situations are stressful for you?
- What do you do when you are stressed? Does this help?
- What else can you do to relieve your stress?
- What are common stress-related physical complaints and illnesses? Do you experience any of these?

MATERIALS: ▶ Large sheets of newsprint, markers.

93
Stress Reduction Through Relaxation

Stage: 3

Challenge: LOW

Grades: ALL

GOALS: ▶
- Evaluate personal stress level
- Learn stress-reducing techniques

DESCRIPTION: ▶ Group members are taught a muscle relaxation exercise as a way to reduce stress in their lives.

DIRECTIONS: ▶ Introduce the concept of stress to the group by asking them for examples of stress-producing situations such as a test, going to a new school, or a parent returning home from a chemical dependence treatment center. Ask them to describe how stress feels and where it locates itself in their bodies, such as a tight stomach or a headache. Then ask them to describe what happens when stress builds up in their bodies (examples might include sleeplessness, stomachaches, and irritability).

Tell the group that you are going to teach them how they can relax their bodies by relaxing their muscles. Point out to them that they can't be relaxed and stressed at the same time, so if they can learn to relax when feeling stressed, the tension will disappear.

Ask everyone to find a comfortable spot on the floor to lie down. They should be flat on their backs, arms at their sides. Remind them that the purpose of this activity isn't to fall asleep but to experience deep relaxation. Now read in a slow, steady voice the **Muscle Relaxation Script** on the following page.

After the relaxation activity is finished, bring the group back together and ask them to discuss how this activity felt. Point out to the group that they can bring about this feeling of deep relaxation more and more quickly if they practice. Once they are proficient with this technique, they can relax their bodies and get rid of stress in many stressful situations, such as before a test, a speech in front of the class, or when things are tense at home.

Ask the group for suggestions as to when they could practice this activity (at night before falling asleep, or for ten minutes after school several times each week).

NOTES: ▶ This activity works best if your group room is carpeted; if not, bring pillows so the hard floor will be bearable. Chairs are the least desirable alternative.

MATERIALS: ▶ **Muscle Relaxation Script**.

Muscle Relaxation Script

❝I am going to give you some instructions that will help you relax your muscles, starting with your arm muscles and ending with the muscles in your legs. For each set of muscles, I'm going to ask you to tighten them for a few seconds and then let them relax. As this happens your body will begin to feel more and more relaxed and your breathing will slow. Remember, though, the goal is to relax your body, not fall asleep. Let your mind wander and drift among peaceful thoughts and enjoy the activity. Let's begin.

Make sure you're in a comfortable position. If you aren't, move around a bit. **(Wait for them to get adjusted.)** Now close your eyes and concentrate on your breathing. Take in a deep breath, deep until you feel your lungs stretch out. And now exhale. Again breathe in deep . . . and then exhale. Feel your heart beat slowing and your body calming. Breathe in deep, deeper . . . and exhale. **(Pause for five seconds.)**

Now I want you to imagine an orange in your right hand. Squeeze this hand tight . . . tight . . . tighter to get every last drop of juice . . . and now drop the orange out of your hand and let your hand fall limp at your side. Notice the difference between the tension and the relaxation. This is how many of the muscles feel in our body when we're stressed and uptight . . . and often without us even realizing it. Now pick up another orange with your right hand and squeeze it, tight . . . tight . . . tighter . . . and then drop the orange and notice your hand feels even more relaxed.

Now let's work on your left hand. **(Repeat with the same instruction as for the right hand.)**

Now you're going to stretch your arm and shoulder muscles by raising your arms up high behind your head. Join your hands together up behind your head and, while keeping them close to the floor, stretch them up behind your head like a cat stretching after an afternoon nap. Feel the tension in you arms and shoulders. Now hold that tight . . . tight . . . tighter . . . and then relax and bring your arms to your sides. Feel how relaxed and limp your arms are now. **(Pause a few seconds and repeat.)**

Now let's focus on your neck muscles. Just like a turtle pulling it's head into it's shell, bring your head down into your shoulders, tight . . . tight . . . tighter . . . and now relax. **(Pause a few seconds and repeat.)**

Now let's relax some of the muscles on your face. I want you to clench your jaw muscles by gritting your teeth together. Feel how tight your jaw muscles get when you do this? Clench them tight now . . . tight . . . tighter . . . and now relax and feel your jaw sag **(Pause a few seconds and then repeat.)**

Oftentimes, our stomachs can get knotted up when we are feeling stress, so let's relax the muscles in the middle of our body. Imagine yourself about to be punched in the stomach and so you make your stomach muscles very tight. Hold it tight . . . tight . . . tighter . . . and now relax. Take a few slow deep breaths now, breathing in deep and then exhale . . . again breath in . . . and exhale. Now tighten your stomach again . . . tight . . . tight . . . tighter . . . and now relax. Again concentrate on your breathing. You're feeling very relaxed now. Your body is heavy; your muscles loose and very relaxed. Your breathing very slow and steady.

Now let's concentrate on your leg muscles. Starting with your right leg, I want you to tighten these muscles by stretching your leg out as far as it will go. Imagine that you are making yourself another foot taller because your leg is stretching out so far. Hold these muscles tight . . . tight . . . tighter . . . and now let them relax. **(Pause a few seconds and repeat.)**

Now let's do the same thing with your left leg. Tighten your left thigh muscle tight . . . tight . . . tighter . . . and then relax **(Pause a few seconds and repeat.)**

Your feet also have lots of muscles that need relaxing. Clench the muscles of your right foot by imagining yourself picking up a softball by grabbing it underneath your toes. Hold your right foot muscles tight . . . tight . . . tighter . . . and now let them relax. **(Pause a few seconds and repeat.)**

And now let's finish with your left foot. Pick up a softball with your toes and hold these muscles tight . . . tight . . . tighter . . . and then let them relax. **(Pause a few seconds and repeat.)**

Now let's return to your breathing. Feel how slow and steady your chest rises and falls. Your body feels so heavy and your muscles so loose. Pure relaxation! Now I'll be quiet and give you a few minutes to enjoy this feeling. Let your mind drift and your breathing slow and I will speak again in a few minutes. **(Give the group a few minutes to enjoy their relaxation.)** **"**

Section H:
Group Challenge Activities

Support groups are about helping students reach out and connect with each other. The activities in this section provide challenges that must be met as a group. This teamwork is especially healing and nurturing for young people whose parents are chemically dependent. Some of the activities go a step further by giving them an outlet for expressing themselves and their thoughts and feelings about parental chemical dependence. These activities give them a voice, a channel, turning their accustomed passive, reactive role into one of taking charge and of empowerment.

94
The Chemical Dependence Adventure Game

Stage: 2-3
Challenge: LOW
Grades: 7-9

GOALS:
- Provide a creative outlet for expression of feelings
- Encourage ability to laugh at personal problems
- Promote teamwork and problem-solving

DESCRIPTION: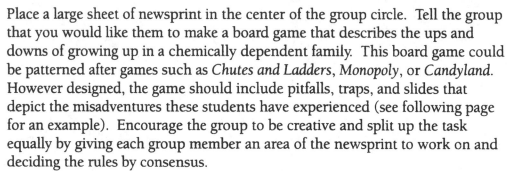
Students create a board game depicting growing up in a chemically dependent family.

DIRECTIONS:
Place a large sheet of newsprint in the center of the group circle. Tell the group that you would like them to make a board game that describes the ups and downs of growing up in a chemically dependent family. This board game could be patterned after games such as *Chutes and Ladders*, *Monopoly*, or *Candyland*. However designed, the game should include pitfalls, traps, and slides that depict the misadventures these students have experienced (see following page for an example). Encourage the group to be creative and split up the task equally by giving each group member an area of the newsprint to work on and deciding the rules by consensus.

Once a rough version of the board game has been designed, give them a piece of posterboard and colored markers. Now, using the newsprint as a guide, they can construct a permanent copy.

During the following session of group, the students can play the game.

NOTES:
If you have more than one support group of this type, you could swap games between the two groups. With the group's permission, you may wish to save this game as an activity for future support groups.

MATERIALS:
Newsprint, posterboard, markers, dice, index cards (in case they want a draw-card pile), objects that can serve as player markers (coins, bottle caps, colored wooden squares).

The Chemical Dependence Adventure Game

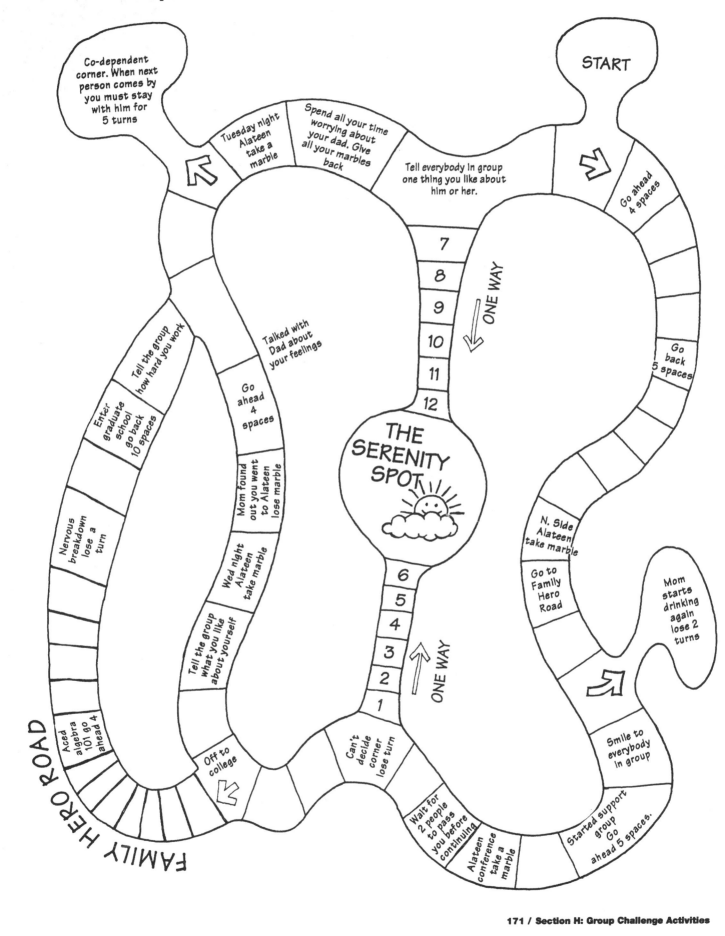

171 / Section H: Group Challenge Activities

95
Poster Promotion

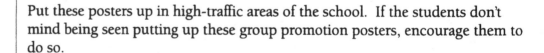

Stage: 3-4
Challenge: LOW
Grades: ALL

GOALS:

- Encourage students to clarify the personal importance of attending a support group
- Promote support groups to the entire student body

DESCRIPTION:

Group members make support group promotional posters to place around the school.

DIRECTIONS:

Ask group members to share how they first felt when they were invited to join a support group. Since most of them will mention feelings of embarrassment, uneasiness, and fear, point out to them that, because of similar feelings, many other students with chemically dependent parents are hesitant to join support groups. Explain to them that you would like the group to make several posters that advertise the purpose of a support group, what happens in a group, what benefits students will receive, and who new students can contact if they are interested. Give them large sheets of poster paper, paints, and markers and let them work in teams or separately as they wish.

NOTES:

Put these posters up in high-traffic areas of the school. If the students don't mind being seen putting up these group promotion posters, encourage them to do so.

MATERIALS:

Poster paper, paints, markers, masking tape.

96
Group Video

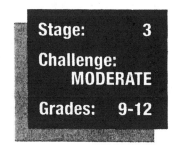

Stage: 3
Challenge: MODERATE
Grades: 9-12

GOALS:

- Increase awareness of the effects of parental chemical dependence on their children
- Provide opportunities for group members to express their concerns and frustrations

DESCRIPTION:

Group members make a short video dramatizing what it's like to grow up in a home with a chemically dependent parent.

DIRECTIONS:

The first step is to write a script. One student should record the ideas as the rest of the group discusses possibilities for the video script. It will be helpful first to choose a focused, specific topic such as what you can do to take care of yourself if you have a chemically dependent parent, or what school-based support groups are all about.

After the script is written, character roles should be assigned to the group members and the script rehearsed until students are comfortable with their parts. The video can then be taped by either a group member or group leader.

NOTES:

This project should not describe any group member's family specifically; instead, the activity encourages the group to dramatize common feelings and problems. In addition, it will be easier and emotionally safer for the students to portray character roles that are not the same as their real-life roles.

This isn't an activity to use in a support group with time constraints. Typically, you should allow for three group sessions to complete this project. Also keep in mind that the main purpose of this activity is to provide a constructive outlet for students to express their concerns, not to make a slick, professional video. The process, not the product, is what's important. This tape should not be shown outside of group.

MATERIALS:

Video equipment such as a camera, tripod, tapes, VCR, monitor.

97
The Student Take-over

Stage: 2, 3

Challenge: MODERATE

Grades: ALL

GOALS:

- Encourage students to take responsibility for their group
- Encourage students to think about their needs

DESCRIPTION:

Group members are given the opportunity to plan and then facilitate the following week's group session.

DIRECTIONS:

Inform the group that during the next week of group they are to be in charge. This means deciding what the focus should be, what activity they should use, how they will divide responsibilities, and what materials they need. Help them plan the group session by addressing these questions in a constructive order.

First off, they need to decide what is an important group topic for them by discussing what it is that they need. Typical examples might include talking more about their feelings, learning how to handle anger, or discussing specific problems they all experience at home.

Next, they should find an activity that focuses on this topic. They might want to invent their own activity (this should be encouraged), or you could show them this book as well as suggest other ideas. The final step is to decide how to divide the responsibilities for the group activity. The following week of group should be reserved for them to follow through with their plan.

NOTES:

Even though they might be disorganized, resist the temptation to jump in and rescue the group. They'll work it out. And after all, though it might not run smoothly, it's their plan.

MATERIALS:

Activity ideas, if they request them.

98
My Secret Pal

GOALS: ▶
- Encourage group unity
- Build self-esteem
- Encourage students to be observant of others
- Provide evaluation of growth and learning

DESCRIPTION: ▶
Students are anonymously assigned to another member of the group. Everyone's task is to observe their secret pal discretely, and then, after at least several sessions, give their pal his or her observations.

DIRECTIONS: ▶
Write each group member's name on a separate slip of paper and place them in a hat, or face down on a table. Ask group members to draw a slip, but not to share the name they draw with anyone else. After drawing names, tell the group that they are to observe their secret pal during future group sessions, looking for positive changes, such as risks taken or feelings being shared. They should do this discretely, though, so that nobody knows who their secret pal is.

At some point during the last few sessions of the group experience, ask group members to reveal their partner's name and to share what they have observed. A student might have noticed that her partner was shy at first but eventually opened up and started sharing lots of feelings, or a secret pal might have observed that his partner always was helping others and putting everybody at ease.

QUESTIONS:
- What did you notice about your secret pal?
- Did your secret pal suspect you were observing her?
- How has your secret pal changed during the course of this group?

NOTES: ▶
You may wish to make the observation phase of this activity span the entire length of the group experience as the revelation of secret pal identities and the sharing of observations can be a great closing activity. Regardless of how many sessions you elect to span, it is best not to assign secret pals until the group is comfortable and familiar with each other, perhaps no earlier than the third or fourth session.

MATERIALS:
Slips of paper.

99
Group Graffiti

Stage: 2-4

Challenge: LOW

Grades: ALL

GOALS: ▶
- Encourage free expression of thoughts and feelings
- Create group unity

DESCRIPTION: ▶ A large sheet of newsprint is taped to the group room wall for students to draw artwork or express thoughts and feelings.

DIRECTIONS: ▶ Using bulletin board paper or large sheets of newsprint, cover a large area of a wall in the group room. Tell the group that they can write and draw whatever they wish as long as it relates to their thoughts and feelings in connection with the group experience.

NOTES: ▶ If you have different groups that meet in the same room, either use different walls for each or take the murals down after each session. Also keep an eye out for negative or hurtful put-downs that a group member might write on the mural.

Depending on the other uses of your group room and the types of walls, you may wish to allow the group to use a small portion of the actual wall to decorate as a group project. Over the course of many groups and years, the group room wall can become a beautiful patchwork quilt of many different group members and group experiences.

MATERIALS: ▶ Poster paper or newsprint and markers.

100
Group Inventory

GOALS: ▶
- Reflect on the health and progress of the group
- Encourage self-inventory
- Promote positive group dynamics

DESCRIPTION: ▶
Students discuss questions on a checklist in order to assess the health of their support group as a whole.

DIRECTIONS: ▶
Explain to the group that just as we individually need to ask ourselves how we are doing from time to time, so does the group as a whole. Give the **Group Inventory Checklist** (see following page) to a member of the group and ask her to choose a question for the group to discuss. If a group discussion doesn't naturally occur, you may ask each group member in turn to answer the specific question before proceeding with the next question. Let everyone have a chance to choose a question for the group to answer.

NOTES: ▶
As the group leader, it's appropriate for you also to answer questions put to the group. It's best to add your comments after everyone else has spoken except for those occasions when the group is hesitant to share their thoughts about a particular question, such as "Are there cliques in our group?" A bold answer on your part here will encourage the rest of the group to speak out.

MATERIALS: ▶
Group Inventory Checklist.

Group Inventory Checklist

1. Does our group help us?

2. Is our group enjoyable?

3. Do we encourage everyone to participate?

4. Does our group feel safe?

5. Does everyone participate in group, or do some members just take up space?

6. Do our group leaders do a good job at helping us?

7. Are there things we should be talking about but don't?

8. Do we spend too much time on some subjects?

9. Is anyone made fun of in group?

10. Are group rules being broken?

11. Are there cliques in our group?

12. Is there something that the group leader isn't doing that should be done?

13. Do people interrupt each other?

14. Do we volunteer information, or do we wait for the group leader to ask us?

15. What is great about our group?

16. How could we improve our group?

101
Support Group Party

GOALS: ▶
- Celebrate the time spent together in group
- Validate personal work students have accomplished
- Bring about closure to the group

DESCRIPTION: ▶

The group members plan and then have a party during one of the last sessions of group.

DIRECTIONS: ▶

Ask group members to plan a party for the following week of group. This party should take place during one of the last sessions of group, although there might be other times when it would also be appropriate, such as the week before Christmas break. Place most of the responsibility for the party on the group's shoulders. They should decide who will be responsible for bringing music, refreshments, and what will happen during the party, such as playing games or listening to music.

NOTES: ▶

Some groups can't handle unstructured time well. If this is the case in your group, you might ask the group members to plan specific activities for the party.

MATERIALS: ▶

Refreshments, music, games.

Appendix A: Feelings List

afraid	enthusiastic	loved	smug
aggressive	envious	mad	surprised
alarmed	exasperated	miserable	tense
amused	excited	needed	terrified
angry	frightened	nervous	threatened
annoyed	frustrated	obstinate	thrilled
anxious	furious	optimistic	troubled
appreciated	glad	paranoid	uneasy
bitter	guilty	perplexed	unimportant
bored	happy	powerful	unloved
calm	helpless	powerless	unsure
cautious	hopeful	puzzled	wanted
comfortable	hopeless	regretful	worried
concerned	horrified	rejected	worthless
confident	hostile	relieved	worthwhile
confused	hurt	resentful	
contented	inadequate	respected	
crushed	insecure	sad	
disappointed	inspired	safe	
discouraged	irritated	satisfied	
eager	jealous	scared	
elated	joyful	secure	
enraged	lonely	shocked	

Appendix B: Resources

NOTE: ▶ Most of the following materials are available from Hazelden Publishing and Educational Services. Please call us at 1-800-328-9000, or visit our website at www.hazelden.org.

BOOKS: ▶ Anderson, Gary L. *When Chemicals Come to School: The Student Assistance Model.*

Fleming, Martin. *Conducting Support Groups for Students Affected by Chemical Dependence: A Guide for Educators and Other Professionals.*

Fleming, Martin. *101 Activities for Teenagers Recovering from Chemical Dependence.*

Fleming, Martin. *101 Activities for Teenagers at Risk for Chemical Dependence or Other Problems.*

Freeman, Shelley MacKay. *From Peer Pressure to Peer Support: Alcohol/Drug Prevention Through Group Process—A Curriculum for Grades 7-12.*

Jesse, Rosalie Cruise. *Children in Recovery.*

Leite, Evelyn, and Pamela Espeland. *Different Like Me: A Book for Teens Who Worry About Their Parents' Use of Alcohol/Drugs.*

Moe, Jerry, and Peter Ways. *Conducting Support Groups for Elementary Children K-6: A Guide for Educators and Other Professionals.*

Moe, Jerry, and Don Pohlman. *Kids' Power: Healing Games for Children of Alcoholics.*

Schmidt, Teresa, and Thelma Spencer. *Building Trust, Making Friends: Tanya Talks about Chemical Dependence in the Family* (Grades 6-8).

Wilmes, David. *Parenting for Prevention: How to Raise a Child to Say No to Alcohol/Drugs—for Parents, Teachers, and Other Concerned Adults.*

BOOKLETS: ▶ Cloninger, Robert. *Genetic and Environmental Factors Leading to Alcoholism.*

Detachment vs. Intervention: Is There a Conflict?

The Family Enablers.

Leite, Evelyn. *How It Feels to be Chemically Dependent.*

Leite, Evelyn. *Detachment: The Art of Letting Go While Living with an Alcoholic.*

PERIODICALS: *Focus on the Family and Chemical Dependence.* 2119-A Hollywood Blvd., Hollywood, FL 33020.

Student Assistance Journal. 1863 Technology Drive, Troy, MI 48083.

OTHER MATERIALS:

Black, Claudia. *The Stamp Game.* MAC Publishing, 5005 E. 39th Avenue, Denver, CO 80207, (303) 331-0148.

VIDEOS:

Different Like Me: For Teenage Children of Alcoholics. Color, 31 minutes.

A Story about Feelings. Color, 10 minutes.

Where's Shelley? Color, 13 minutes.

My Father's Son: The Legacy of Alcoholism. Color, 33 minutes Gerald T. Rogers Productions, 5225 Old Orchard Road, Suite 23A, Skokie, IL 60077.

Soft is the Heart of a Child. Color, 30 minutes. Hazelden.

Tell Someone: A Music Video. Color, 4 minutes Addiction Counselors Continuing Ed. Services, P.O. Box 30380, Indianapolis, IN 46230.

NATIONAL ORGANIZATIONS:

COAF
Children of Alcoholics Foundation, Inc.
P.O. Box 4185
Grand Central Station
New York, NY 10163
(212) 754-0656

Johnson Institute
7205 Ohms Lane
Minneapolis, MN 55439-2159
(612) 831-1630 or (800) 231-5165

NACoA
National Association for Children of Alcoholics
11426 Rockville Pike, Suite 100
Rockville, MD 20852
(301) 468-0985

NCADD
National Council on Alcoholism and Drug Dependence
12 West 21st Street
New York, NY 10010
(212) 206-6770